CW00956407

HIGH STREET
HEROES

HIGH STREET HEROES

THE STORY OF BRITISH RETAIL IN 50 PEOPLE

JOHN TIMPSON

ICON

Published in the UK in 2015 by
Icon Books Ltd, Omnibus Business Centre,
39–41 North Road, London N7 9DP
email: info@iconbooks.com
www.iconbooks.com

Sold in the UK, Europe and Asia
by Faber & Faber Ltd, Bloomsbury House,
74–77 Great Russell Street,
London WC1B 3DA or their agents

Distributed in the UK, Europe and Asia
by TBS Ltd, TBS Distribution Centre, Colchester Road,
Frating Green, Colchester CO7 7DW

Distributed in the USA by
Consortium Book Sales & Distribution
34 13th Avenue NE, Suite 101
Minneapolis, MN 55413

Distributed in Australia and New Zealand
by Allen & Unwin Pty Ltd,
PO Box 8500, 83 Alexander Street,
Crows Nest, NSW 2065

Distributed in South Africa by
Jonathan Ball, Office B4, The District,
41 Sir Lowry Road, Woodstock 7925

Distributed in Canada by Publishers Group Canada,
76 Stafford Street, Unit 300,
Toronto, Ontario M6J 2S1

ISBN: 978-184831-916-5

Text copyright © 2015 John Timpson

The author has asserted his moral rights

No part of this book may be reproduced in any form, or by any
means, without prior permission in writing from the publisher

Typeset in Epic by Marie Doherty

Printed and bound in the UK by Clays Ltd, St Ives plc

This book is dedicated to the memory of two people who lit my interest in retailing over 55 years ago.

My father got me going with nightly conversations about the business over the washing up (he washed, I dried). Bill Branston, the Timpson shop manager in Altrincham, mentored me for my first three months as a shop assistant. He made me toe the line on the shop floor but when we spent every tea break together he passed on his tips for success.

At eighteen I was hooked; that fascination for retailing is still as strong today.

ABOUT THE AUTHOR

John Timpson CBE was born in 1943 and educated at Oundle and Nottingham University. In 1975 he became Managing Director of William Timpson Ltd, the business that had borne his family name since 1865, and he is now sole owner of the company, which has a turnover in the UK of £200m per year. His previous book was *Ask John* (Icon, 2014), based on his *Daily Telegraph* column of the same name. His book *Upside Down Management* (Wiley, 2010) was described by the *Financial Times* as 'a practical and inspirational manual for anyone who runs a business'. Timpson and his wife Alex have been foster carers for 31 years, during which time they have fostered 90 children. He lives in Cheshire.

CONTENTS

PREFACE

At the beginning of my retailing career, 55 years ago, there were no supermarkets, no out-of-town shopping centres and not even a hint of internet shopping. The high street was full of made-to-measure tailors and traditional grocers. Among the fascias you could find Mac Fisheries, Dewhurst, John Collier and Timothy Whites & Taylors.

I was asked to write about my top 50 retailers, the people I consider have made the biggest difference to UK shopping. My book goes well beyond the original brief. In making my pick I paint a picture of how shops have changed and who has had the biggest influence on the shape of shopping.

Although most commentators recognise the influence of market research, electronic point of sale, computerised stock control and sophisticated shop layout, I clearly see the main agents for change to be those forward-thinking shopkeepers and inspirational entrepreneurs who have led major retailers through a period of such rapid transformation.

At the end of the book I finally reveal my top 50, but along the way I learnt a lot about the characters who have successfully steered their companies through the recent retail revolution.

INTRODUCTION

When I started to write this book I intended to produce a light-hearted survey of my own personal top 50 retailers, but in doing so I got distracted by the bigger picture they painted of shopping in the 20th century. After a lot of detours I finally fulfilled my brief so, if you want to cheat, skip to the last chapter where my list is revealed, but you will miss all the things I discovered along the way. In compiling the list of names and their fascinating stories I learnt a lot about retailing – what works, where companies can fail, and how much has changed over the last 50 and more years.

Those who think we are currently going through a once-in-a-lifetime retail revolution have been misled. The current change in shopping habits is just one more tremor in a long earthquake that was already shaking up the high street when I started work as a shop assistant in 1960.

I was one of twelve people working in the Timpson shoe shop in Railway Street, Altrincham, led by manager Bill Branston (Mr Branston to me). The team included first sales, Mr Williamson, Miss Bruce who did the shoe dyeing, and Miss McCleod who ran the women's and children's floor. We were split by gender: men served men, while women – who were paid at a considerably lower rate – served women and children. Everyone called me 'Mister John'! We all worked Monday to

Saturday, but Wednesday was half-day closing in Altrincham so I left at 1.00pm and went to play golf and bridge with the retired men at Hale Golf Club.

Every customer was given personal service. We brought a selection of shoes from the boxes that lined the wall and, while sitting in front of the customer on a fitting stool, helped them try on each shoe. On a busy Saturday I had to serve three customers at once, write out the sales dockets and wrap up the goods in paper (no Sellotape – we just used string which Mr Branston could snap with his bare hands).

I realised that our Altrincham branch was relatively up to date only when, the next year, my father took me on several days out visiting other shops. Many were in city suburbs, some still surrounded by bomb damage remaining from the blitz: old-fashioned buildings where the manager still lived in the flat above the shop. As we drove round we went through some areas where there were no shops at all. 'That's where old C shop used to be,' said my father as we went through Hulme in Manchester, one of many slum clearance areas where the only buildings left standing were churches and pubs. My great grandfather can't have expected to open lots of shops because he referred to them by letters of the alphabet. His first shop in Oldham Street, Manchester was 'A' and all was fine until his 27th shop was opened in Levenshulme, which was '1'. When we installed our first computer in 1960 the letters had to go, so 'A' shop became 250 and 'C' was 252 for a few months before it was closed.

By 1960, city centres like Coventry, Plymouth and Southampton that had been severely damaged during the Second World War were rebuilt with characterless concrete buildings and pedestrian precincts. The local independent shopkeeper couldn't afford the high rents demanded for these new shops so the shopping centres were filled with national multiple retailers. It wasn't just the big cities that had newly built pedestrian shopping. Local authority developments popped up all over the country, often taking trade from the local community. Old streets were demolished by property developers who built new enclosed shopping centres. The first American-style precincts were the Arndale Centres, developed by Arnold Hagenbach, a baker, and Sam Chippendale, a property developer. They opened 23 centres between 1961 and 1975, which included Luton, Stretford, Wandsworth, Middleton and Manchester city centre. They, and others who copied them, changed the shape of our high streets and collected criticism along the way. As one commentator said, 'All the old buildings – good, bad and indifferent – are replaced with chain stores, supermarkets and flats devoid of distinction, all looking alike, systematically destroying our historic centres.'

These new shopping developments gave ambitious multiple shopkeepers the perfect chance to expand, while some of the more conservative family firms were left with a portfolio of shops in declining locations. Most well-established multiple retailers had a significant number of freeholds, which became the target for acquisitive competitors like Charles Clore and Isaac Wolfson. The 1960s and 70s saw a lot of takeover activity and the development of several store groups including UDS, Sears and Burton whose big buying power brought more competitive pressure on smaller shopkeepers.

Retailers have always watched the Budget with their fingers crossed. In one phrase the Chancellor can make a significant change to our profit margins. From 1940 until 1973 the main game-changer was purchase tax, which not only could alter from budget to budget but also had different rates for different classes of goods or services, at times ranging from 0 per cent to 100 per cent. Its successor VAT has been less volatile but is now double the introductory rate of 10 per cent.

While we were watching purchase tax and VAT, the government made a major difference to retailing with the introduction of two more unlikely measures. The abolition of resale price maintenance by Edward Heath in 1964 paved the way for the price cutters and in particular accelerated the development of out-of-town supermarkets at the expense of your local corner shop. The savings now available on branded goods made a drive to an out-of-town supermarket well worthwhile.

The other government measure was a case of unintended consequences. In 1975, with inflation approaching 27 per cent, the Wilson government, keen to agree some sort of incomes policy with the unions, agreed an across-the-board maximum pay increase of £6 a week with all but a guarantee that this would be given to the lowest paid. At this time our shoe shop assistants were earning about £12 a week, so the government gave them an increase of around 50 per cent. Our wage bill rose so sharply we had to cut staffing levels, which reduced the level of service in shops and accelerated the introduction of self-service.

The other traumatic but fortunately short-lived result of government action was in 1972 during the miners' strike when non-essential businesses (service industries like shops rather than factories) could use power for only three days a week. A few got through with their own generators, and our shoe repair outlets escaped any restriction by claiming to be a factory, but the rest simply shut up shop for half the week. Turnover was lost, but nothing like as much as had been expected (makes you wonder whether our ancestors weren't right to close on Sundays and half a day during the week!).

It was the freehold property portfolio that persuaded UDS to buy Swears & Wells, the first business where I was given the chance to be chief executive. The 60 shops that I ran for a couple of years included two freeholds on Oxford Street, London. As a multiple specialising in selling fur coats it could never afford the market rent, and when the business was closed down, five years later, the two freeholds were sold for more money than the whole 60-shop chain had made in profit over the previous decade.

Gradually over the last 50 years the ownership of high street freeholds has passed from the retailers to insurance companies and pension funds. The new landlords ruled the roost for decades, demanding 25-year leases with five-year, upwards only, rent reviews and a draconian approach to covenants and dilapidations. It is only since 2008 that the retailers have had some chance of revenge, although a softening of rental values has been partially offset by a significant increase in business rates.

The Sainsburys, Ian MacLaurin of Tesco, and the double act of Archie Norman and Allan Leighton at Asda all brought a bit of America to the UK when developing their supermarket strategy but, despite the reputation of US retail, the British high street is mostly home-grown – perhaps we are still the nation of shopkeepers.

Trips to visit Walmart, Safeway, Piggly Wiggly and many more stateside stores have been essential research, but without any outside help our supermarket sector would still have created one of the biggest seismic shifts in shopping habits, far greater than the changes so far created by internet shopping. Ask your local butcher, baker or fishmonger (if you still have one) whether the out-of-town competition made any difference.

One American import that caused a considerable stir was trading stamps. By the time Sperry & Hutchinson stamps had crossed the Atlantic, Green Shield were already established in the UK, so the S&H stamps had to turn from green to pink. It was a new and significant way to give a discount, especially before resale price maintenance was abolished. Things got a lot worse for the downtrodden independent grocer when Tesco scrapped Green Shield Stamps over a weekend and launched stunning price cuts across the store.

During the 1970s, customers started to realise that they were expected to do more of the work: self-service had arrived and was here to stay. For some of us it was an unwelcome change. I used to drive past petrol stations until I could find one with forecourt assistance. This was before the cost of motoring took away so much of the family budget that it seriously affected every other category of spending. In 1963 only 35 per cent of households had a car and I could fill up my Morris Minor for less than £1.

The increase in self-service wasn't just in supermarkets. Shoe shops, fashion stores, Boots and W.H. Smith all swapped counters for checkouts and customer service suffered, but not due to a lack of training. It was a time when business spent more on training than ever before. Every extra pound on the training budget brought savings in tax or extra grants from the government. Most multiple shops opened half-an-hour late once a week to hold group customer care courses. This led to the bizarre situation of customers knocking on the door desperate to be served, only to see the notice:

'Shop closed for training – to improve the service we give our customers.'

We installed our first computer in 1961, making Timpson one of the pioneers. It was an enormous piece of kit, filling a large air-conditioned office with a series of magnetic tapes on disk calculating throughout the night simply to update a day's stock movements in our warehouse. I expect today's iPhones have the capacity to do the job in less than a second.

We might have been an early starter but several retailers were ahead of the game, particularly Sainsbury's, who saw the importance of computerisation before other food retailers, and Mothercare, where founder and chief executive Selim Zilkha was the first to create a comprehensive stock control system in the clothing industry. We were keen to follow in their footsteps, believing the advice given by our computer sales team who claimed: 'Computerisation will reduce your stock holding, and give quicker and more reliable sales statistics. The result will be higher turnover, lower costs and a better margin.' We have upgraded our computer system several times, on each occasion installing smaller and much more powerful technology. We now can't envisage how we survived with a paper-driven system, and have certainly cut our costs (we used to have 40 girls adding up our weekly sales figures), but we are still looking for many of the other benefits promised by a succession of computer salesmen.

By 1980 the new business schools were starting to believe that retailing is a science not an art. The idea of retail engineering, backed up by the enormous amount of data and customers' details produced by electronic sales capture, drove a new generation of retail executives to spend their time in head office, planning the perfect shopping experience. The electronic point of sale (EPOS) tills gave head office control over prices and a team of central merchandisers could control stock levels. Instead of placing orders, local shop managers were told what to stock and where and how to display it. Unsurprisingly, a lot of companies lost the personal touch, senior management seldom visited their shops and individual customers didn't get so much personal service.

All retailers had to face up to both new regulations and deregulation. Health and safety and employment law improved the way shops were operated, but the changes came at a cost. Many of the buildings put up during the concrete reconstruction of town centres in the 1950s and 60s used asbestos, high alumina cement and other materials that subsequently proved suspect. These blighted buildings lost their freehold value until restored by expensive maintenance. New buildings had to provide disabled access and the 1992 Workplace (Health, Safety and Welfare) regulations stipulated the need for separate lavatories for men and women. We had two health and safety issues that curbed sales at Timpson. In the shoe shops we used an X-ray machine to measure children's feet – most of the kids loved the machines, and so did the mums until they discovered the potential harm from exposure to radiation. In our shoe repair factories we had to discontinue our Nu Shade service – shoe re-colouring which took place in special spray booths outside the back door. The colour change was very successful and at 7/9d (39p) a pair was very popular with customers, but part of the pleasure our colleagues got from doing the job came from what is now known as substance abuse. Nu Shade was discontinued.

Wage rates have risen dramatically. I was lucky to start on £5.7.6d (£5.38) a week. If I had been a girl, my basic weekly wage would have been less than £4. Equal pay made a big difference to retailers, especially in those sectors where the majority of shop assistants were women. More recently working time directives have increased the amount of overtime and the statutory minimum rate of pay has created a significant increase in the overall rate of pay for shop workers.

The main deregulation that changed our retail landscape was Sunday trading. When the topic was being debated before a vote in the Commons it was quite clear that this was a battle between the big boys, particularly the supermarkets, and the small local trader. It would take a much bigger percentage cost increase for a small shop to open on a Sunday than for the big supermarket down the road.

With shoe repair shops that might employ only two people, or even one, we were bound to be a loser, so I signed up to the Keep Sunday Special Campaign and paraded outside Parliament with a banner that said 'Cobblers to Sunday Shopping'. We lost, and costs increased throughout the whole of retail.

Traditional high street shops faced increased competition from mail order companies. The biggest catalogues – Littlewoods, Grattan, Freemans, Kay, and British Mail Order – sold nearly 10 per cent of all clothing and footwear in the UK, a figure yet to be overtaken by internet sales, so the threat of online shopping has a fairly familiar feel. For retailers of big ticket items like furniture, carpets, bedding and electricals, the new competition came from retail parks, which grew rapidly with anchor tenants like B&Q, Comet, Halfords, MFI, Allied Carpets, Homebase and Focus. This development pretty well took these trades off the high street, where we no longer see Cyril Lord Carpets or the Local Electricity Board shops.

Perhaps one of the biggest but least acknowledged changes over the last 50 years has been the steady demise of the traditional markets. There are still several thriving market halls up and down the country. There continues to be a buzz about the busy markets in Swansea and Leeds, but more and more empty stalls are appearing in Abingdon Street market, Blackpool, and the markets in Hereford and Halifax. Many of our major retailers were developed by market stall holders who expanded into a wider world, like Jack Cohen of Tesco and, indeed, Michael Marks of M&S. The market traders are now competing with Primark, Poundland, B&M Bargains and Sports Direct, which can buy and sell at much lower prices.

Retailers looking for new sites, and estate agents trying to sell them, use Goad plans. These maps give a bird's-eye view of a retail centre, showing the fascia name of every unit on the street. The plans are named after Charles E. Goad, who first produced street plans to help insurance companies assess fire risk. The Goad company, now part of Experian, started producing these shopping plans in 1966 so the earlier editions provide a Who's Who of the 1960s high street. Some stalwarts have survived, such as W.H. Smith, Boots, M&S and Russell & Bromley, but most have disappeared. The old names are still familiar to my generation but most of today's shoppers would wonder 'who was that and what did they do?' Here are a few names to test your memory: Paige, John Collier, Timothy Whites & Taylors, Dewhurst, Dunns, J Hepworth & Son, Trueform, Our Price, Kardomah, Richard Shops, Rediffusion, Home and Colonial, MacFisheries, Bewlays, Van Allan, Weaver to Wearer, Fine Fare and Liptons. Some of these names were axed following an acquisition. Most of the stores that are now called Debenhams or House of Fraser set off with much more interesting names, like Swan & Edgar or Arding and Hobbs. Greggs and Johnsons were two of the few multiple chains that retained the original names of their takeover targets, so for years you could still trade with Baker's Oven, Thurstons and Prices. For many years after being bought by Johnsons the Cleaners you could continue to take your suit to Harton Clean, Zernys, Smiths and Pullars of Perth. The only other business I can recall that allowed newly acquired subsidiaries such autonomy was Allied Shoe Repairs, whose chain of shoe repair shops traded as Malones, Paynes, Shoecraft and Modern Shoe Repairs until they were sold in 1985 to Mr Minit, who changed every fascia. Now they are all called Timpson. Others that were rebranded include J Hepworth & Son that became Next, Timothy Whites & Taylors that became Boots, and Tandy that was turned into Carphone Warehouse.

Some businesses catered for a declining market and were eventually bound to fail. The men's tailoring chains including John Collier and Alexandre Ltd, which almost totally sold to the made-to-measure suit market, never adapting to the demand for ready-to-wear casual fashion. Radio Rentals, Granada and Martin Dawes were businesses born because almost everyone rented their television. Singer had a chain of sewing machine shops when home dressmaking was widespread, and although our weather hasn't changed, the sales at Kendall Rainwear and their competitor Direct Raincoat suffered when fewer people walked to work or waited at bus stops. Blockbuster could never survive the competition from the internet and films on demand.

Here's a game you can play to pass the time waiting at an airport or driving down the motorway. Name chains of shops that have disappeared in the last twenty years. There are enough to keep you going for the length of the M1, but I will just give you twenty to start you off: C&A, Littlewoods, Foster Brothers, Woolworths, Phones4U, JJB Sports, Comet, Borders, Zavvi, MFI, Threshers, Past Times, Barratts, La Senza, Adams Childrenswear, Dolcis, Jane Norman, Oddbins, Viyella and Virgin Megastore.

Although retailers who failed to survive all the changes in government policy and our shopping habits often found someone or something else to blame for failure, most of their problems were self-inflicted.

Some years ago a university business school study into family-owned companies found that family firms were an inefficient drain on the economy. On closer inspection this was naive academic nonsense. Nearly every retail company has started as a small family business and there are plenty of examples like Kwik Fit, DFS and Iceland to prove that the family founder can do a much better job than a professional manager. Nor do I, as a fourth-generation cobbler, subscribe to the inevitability of clogs to clogs in three generations. Fenwicks, Russell & Bromley and, for many years, Clarks have shown how to create success by keeping it in the family, but none of these businesses can match Berry Brothers. Founded in 1698 and acquired by the Berry family in the early 1800s, the company is now run by a member of the seventh generation, Simon Berry.

If anyone is surprised that family ownership can create such success, they should read a letter my grandfather wrote to our shops in 1955 when, at the age of 75, he apologised that 'following my recent illness I feel I will no longer be able to continue my habit of trying to visit every shop during each year. I miss meeting you all and hearing how you would like us to develop your business. It feels like a long time since I met some of you but I was surprised to discover that I have visited over 120 shops in the last twelve months.' I have discovered that family ownership, in the right hands, is a very helpful management tool.

Several top retailers have found it difficult to pass control to a new management team. M&S and Sainsbury's in the late 1990s and, more recently, both Tesco and Morrisons have shown that it can be difficult for a new team to develop the strategy and keep the old culture. Perhaps companies can get too big. Burtons was fine until it hit a tough trading period, UDS was certainly too complicated for the management talent available, and the Sears team under Liam Strong was too short of retail experience to run such a wide spread of retail shops.

Woolworths and Littlewoods simply failed to keep up to date and showed the signs left by years of cost control by head office. When we at Timpson owned Sketchley, I particularly remember visiting their shop in London Road, Brighton in 2004, and being told that the only time the shop had been decorated in twenty years was in 1999 when the manager, her husband and their two children tackled the job over a weekend. Head office-controlled cost-cutting went so far at Sketchley that the branch staff were not allowed to pay for window cleaners or buy postage stamps. If they wanted to send a letter they had to order the stamps from head office and the stamps were sent to them in the post.

C. Northcote Parkinson was right. Over time, organisations tend to gather more managers and central management becomes an end in itself. In recent years Tesco has suffered from a bloated head office which dictated policy in detail without being totally in touch with the shops. My guess is that they, and many other big retailers, have had at least two tiers of management too many that spent a lot of their time playing business politics and sitting in meetings designed to use joined-up thinking to agree policy. These organisations will benefit from having fewer executives and more common sense.

When the founding entrepreneur hands the business over to a team of professional managers, there is a danger that the flair that created success is replaced by a complicated process that hopes to keep up the momentum with a set of rules and key performance indicators.

This does not mean that once the company gets into the hands of a new management team it is doomed to failure. There are plenty of examples of inspirational leaders who took on a well-established company and made it better. Ralph Halpern, Terry Leahy, Stuart Rose, Simon Wolfson and Justin King all come into this category, big personalities who put their personal stamp on a big business. These entrepreneurs have made a major contribution to shaping the character of today's shopping, but you don't need to have a big business to be called a high street hero. All over the country there are fantastic independents with just one shop: butchers, fashion retailers, farm shops and interior designers that ooze excellence. The big retailers should always be on the lookout for new ideas and they can often be found in small shops that dare to be different. If I ran a deli I would copy Percy Grantham in Alderley Edge, who sets a gold standard for others to follow.

Most of our best known retailers were started by one person opening a market stall or a small shop. M&S, Sainsbury's, Dixons and Boots were all developed by families that turned a successful shop into a national chain. No list of retail heroes would be complete without including Jesse Boot, Ken Morrison and Simon Marks.

If I look back at those Goad plans, with over 75 per cent of the fascias no longer in business, we must be thankful for all the new retail concepts that have been developed over the last 50 years. Without them our shopping centres would be full of empty units. Anita Roddick, Charles Dunstone, Mike Ashley and Julian Metcalfe have produced The Body Shop, Carphone Warehouse, Sports Direct and Pret a Manger. Most of these ventures seemed unlikely candidates for national success but few can have been given less chance of survival than Ann Summers, which has been driven to success by Jacqueline Gold, and the bluntly named Supercigs chain, started on Wolverhampton market and sold for £530m. For a time Supercigs was owned by Tesco, but not many people know that.

Most new retail ideas face rapid failure. In the 1960s a lot of the little shops selling jeans in expensive sites didn't last too long, and a number of fashion shops like Miss Attitude followed them into oblivion, but the brilliantly named Manchester fashion store Stolen From Ivor started by selling Levi jeans at £2.7.6d (£2.38) a pair and had customers carrying their 'Stolen From Ivor' bags all over Manchester. The chain grew to 43 stores; but the Stockport store is the only one still open for business.

Some ideas didn't last so long. Most of the fish foot spas disappeared within a couple of years, and I wonder how long specialist e-cigarette shops will be around. But my prize for the shortest lived, unluckiest retail concept goes to a shop in the Westgate Arcade, Peterborough called Just Eggs. It was the age of niche retailing, with plenty of publicity and high share prices being achieved by Tie Rack and Sock Shop. The egg shop sold brown eggs, white eggs and eggs in a range of pastel shades. There were hens' eggs, duck eggs and quails' eggs – any sort of eggs you could think of, but nothing else. Four weeks after the shop opened, Edwina Currie made her ministerial announcement about salmonella, demand for eggs dived and within three months Just Eggs had closed.

Some chains just got battered by their opposition. Sports Direct won the battle with JJB Sports by cutting prices and opening next door. Card Factory caused Clinton Cards to go into receivership just by doing a much better job in much smaller shops with much lower rents.

Happily, there are enough growth businesses to keep shopping alive. We are seeing more fast food with Costa, Pret a Manger, Caffè Nero, Patisserie Valerie and Subway. Many are able to expand quickly through franchising, which has helped the growth of one of the big success stories: Specsavers. New fashion formats will continue to emerge in the wake of current favourites Cath Kidston, Jack Wills, AllSaints and Hollister, a shop so dark inside that older people like me can't see the merchandise.

As you will have gathered from this introduction, the search for my top 50 retail heroes has taken me on an unplanned stroll through 50-plus years of UK shopkeeping, but I didn't go everywhere and some possible heroes may be miffed that I passed them by. In particular I have left the online retailers for another day, on the basis that most of them have yet to prove that they can make money. When the dot-com bubble burst just after the millennium, I thought that investors had seen sense and would never again value companies on an inflated extrapolation of dreams. But it has happened once more. AO.com floated on 200 times earnings, making a business with sales of £275 million worth an initial listed price of

£1.2 billion. Amazon, which has yet to make a profit, has a market capitalisation of $174 billion. The original favourite, lastminute.com, made only a modest profit of £200,000 three years after floating at a market value of £571 million. It has been suggested that the combined online business done by the big supermarkets creates a loss of £100 million. It can't be cheap to pick every individual order from the warehouse shelves, and the Tesco driver has to be pretty slick to deliver to enough doors an hour to make home delivery a profitable proposition.

I hope Max Spielmann makes money out of Click and Collect, which I'm pretty sure is the way that Next and John Lewis are making home shopping worthwhile, but I'm not ready to put an e-retailer into my list of heroes. They may well feature on a future list though, alongside some, as yet, totally unknown names, because over half the most successful retailers of 2025 almost certainly have not yet been created.

When I started writing I had no idea how I was going to pick the order of my top 50 retail heroes, so I decided to delay the choice until I had written about all the candidates. By then, I realised I'd been set an almost impossible task. Rating the merits of Jack Cohen against Simon Wolfson or choosing the better of Charles Dunstone and Jesse Boot is as difficult as comparing Jack Hobbs with Ian Botham or Rory McIlroy with Sam Snead. It might be possible to pick between Ken Morrison and Terry Leahy because they both ran supermarkets at the same time but it isn't fair to pitch Julian Richer against Ralph Halpern or Terence Conran against Harry Selfridge.

After a lot of anguish I made life easy by taking my top 50 and putting each name on a separate card, which I happily shuffled around for four hours until I felt I had put them in the right order. As I said, the result is at the end of the book. It is up to you whether you want to cheat and look at the list before joining my trip round the world of retail. But perhaps it might be more fun to skip through the book first and then see if you agree with my conclusions.

46 YEARS ON

When people reach my age (I can't believe I'm 72 already) they often have a distorted view of the past. I was talking to James, my son and chief executive, about how much the high street was changing even before he was born (1971) and I could tell by his quizzical expression that he didn't believe me. So, to put my memory to the test, I acquired Goad's street trader plans of Peterborough and Oxford for both 1968 and 2014. The comparison sharpened up my memory and showed that 46 years is a long time on the high street.

Since the Co-op department store in Peterborough was bought by Beales a few years ago, the only fascia that remains on the same premises in the centre of the city is M&S. Every other shop that was trading 47 years ago has been either sold, closed, moved or knocked down to build the Queensgate Centre.

The Peterborough map for 1968 is full of memories. Granada and Radio Rentals recall the days when most televisions were rented. Finlays the tobacconist supplied customers who were allowed to smoke inside the centrally located Odeon and Embassy cinemas. The Singer Sewing Machine shop and Cyril Lord Carpets ('This is luxury you can afford – by Cyril Lord') were soon to disappear. Singer Sewing Machine shops were already closing across the country and Cyril Lord collapsed in November 1968 due to, according to a report at the time, 'the founder Cyril Lord's unbridled innovation, inadequate product testing, lack of market research and uncontrolled advertising budget'.

There were thirteen shoe shops all well located – Freeman Hardy Willis, Dolcis, Trueform, Hilton, Turners, John Plant, Lotus, Barratts, Bata, Easiephit, Manfield, Briggs and Shoefayre – none of these footwear chains have survived.

Today, retail experts talk about supermarkets moving back into town with their convenience stores. But, in 1968, plenty of food multiples were trading in the middle of Peterborough – David Greig, Lipton, International Stores, Maypole, Fine Fare and George Mason along with MacFisheries and Dewhurst the butcher, owned by the Vestey family.

Tesco is trading in almost the same spot, having moved next door into a property that was previously a garage (the original Tesco building is now a Yates' Wine Lodge). This store was where we opened our worst Tesco/Timpson concession and it was all my fault. When I inspected the site I was in such a rush I never noticed the two cut-price cobblers on the market nearby. We never had a chance.

The Goad plans don't just map movements in shopping habits, they also show how society has changed. Across the road from Tesco the premises once used by the WVS are now occupied by Wetherspoons, next door to Quicksilver amusements, which was previously Top Rank Bingo – and no doubt, had the right sort of user clause to allow slot machines into the city centre.

Like most big shopping centres Peterborough had plenty of department stores. Family businesses all with a fascinating history – Sheltons, Fairways, Farrons, Brierleys and Armstrongs.

All these names have disappeared, replaced by the John Lewis store, built as part of the Queensgate Centre. Perhaps the most surprising feature on the old street map was the number of building societies. People in Peterborough had plenty of mutual societies fighting for their business. There was the Anglia Building Society, The Peterborough, Peterborough General, Co-op Permanent, Leeds Permanent, Abbey National, West Bromwich, Bedfordshire and The Bradford and Bingley (whose massive office building was being knocked to the ground when I last visited our Timpson and Max shops in Bingley). Now there are more pay day loan shops than building societies.

Oxford's shopping streets haven't changed quite as much. The Post Office still trades from the same site, but probably has a much longer queue, as will almost certainly be the case at W.H. Smith, which occupies the same site but has expanded next door. M&S has moved from Cornmarket to a property formerly occupied by the Co-op on Queen Street. The old M&S site is now split between Next, Fat Face, River Island, Carphone Warehouse and Superdrug. Woolworths has become Gap and Zara, and Littlewoods was demolished in 1983 to create room for The Clarendon Centre. Shortly after my 1968 street plan was printed a few shops disappeared to make way for The Westgate Centre that was built in 1972. The Westgate is due to be completely rebuilt before 2018, showing that even new shopping centres can't be expected to last more than 50 years.

Boots is now three times the size but still trades on Cornmarket Street where Austin Reed continues to be a neighbour.

I'm pleased to see that The Randolph Hotel and St Michael's Church have avoided the developers' bulldozer but just about every other building is home to a different business compared with 47 years ago, apart from the banks. But most banks have changed their name. Today we bank with Santander, HSBC, NatWest, Barclays, Lloyds TSB and Royal Bank of Scotland. In 1968 there was Martins Bank, The Midland, Williams Deacons, Westminster Bank and The National Provincial.

The Southern Gas Showroom and the Southern Electricity Service Shop both occupied big sites where customers paid their weekly and monthly bills. Like the Eastern Gas and Electricity Boards in Peterborough, these shops were Currys' major competitors.

All the womenswear chains then in Oxford are now extinct – Paige, Peter Richards, Wetherall, Noel Fashions, Kendall Rainwear and Etam. The Oxford public could pick from plenty of multiple tailors – Jackson & Son, John Collier, Foster Brothers, Hector Powe, J Hepworth & Son, Dunns and, the only ones still trading, Burton and Austin Reed. Dunns was founded in 1886 by George Arthur Dunn who started selling hats on the streets of Birmingham and built up a chain of 200 shops simply selling men's hats. You only have to see pictures of people over 50 years ago to see how a men's hat shop could make money. Well-dressed men had a hat for every occasion – top hats, a trilby, bowler hats, deerstalkers, pork pie and panama hats, straw hats and flat caps. Dunns diversified into suits, blazers and sports jackets but it remained a business with an old-fashioned image, which remained stuck in the past until it closed down in 1996.

Oxford in 1968 had most of the household names that seemed to be permanent fixtures: Timothy Whites & Taylors, The Scotch Wool Shop, J Lyons, Salisbury's Handbags and Timpson shoes.

The Timpson shop on Queen Street, together with the shop next door and restaurant above, was part of our company's freehold portfolio. My grandfather bought the building in the 1930s for about £50,000.

In 1983, when I was trying to do a management buyout, 33–35 Queen Street, Oxford became more important than I'd ever imagined. Most of the funding had to come from selling freeholds and leasing them back. We needed to sell £30m of property to do the deal, the building in Oxford was valued at £3.75m, over 120 times what my grandfather paid and more than 12 per cent of the money I had to raise. We did the deal, which was key to securing the buyout.

Four years later with too many shoe shops on the high street and lots of other shops selling shoes, I found it so difficult to make money I decided to sell our shoe shops. So, in 1987, the Timpson shoe shop on Queen Street, Oxford became Oliver Shoes, which quickly sold the lease. The whole of that site now trades as Miss Selfridge.

When the street map of Oxford was compiled in 1968 I would never have guessed how much shopping would change over the next 46 years and certainly would not have expected Timpson shoes to be one of the earliest names to disappear. We were almost the first shoe chain to sell out; over 90 per cent of the other shoe retailers followed in our footsteps.

If you live long enough to see the shape of shopping in 2061, look back at the street plans for 2014. Almost everything will have changed and the success stories will still have been written by inspirational people, who will form another generation of Heroes on the High Street.

THE SUPERMARKETS

Whenhen my mother took me shopping her favoured suppliers included Mr Hulme the butcher in Hale Barns (no one used his Christian name) and Cadman's the grocer in Hale, a shop that smelt of freshly ground coffee which, like the sugar, was weighed to order and wrapped in brown paper. We didn't need a supermarket trolley, Mr Cadman delivered to our house.

We were lucky, we had a car while most walked or went by bus – this was 1950, before the first out-of-town superstores came to the UK. But even then it would have been possible to predict that shopping planned around the motor car, which was already part of life in the USA, would one day come to the UK, but no one could have guessed which of the food retailers would grow to dominate the market and which would disappear. The present supermarket scene was shaped by a small number of leaders who turned their chain of food shops into the four supermarkets that by 2010 controlled over 70 per cent of UK food retailing.

TESCO

Jack Cohen

Jack Cohen, the son of a Polish immigrant tailor, started working as an apprentice tailor but after being demobbed from the First World War, during which he served in France for the Royal Flying Corps, he started a market stall in Hackney selling surplus stock bought from the NAAFI. Before long he had a number of stalls and a wholesale business. The Tesco name didn't appear until 1924 – a brand created from the initials of his tea supplier, T.E. Stockwell and the first two letters of his surname. Jack took market trading to the high street with open fronted shops following his philosophy of 'Pile it high, sell it cheap'. He was keen to expand and clearly had a good eye for property, often having the courage to be the first to open in a newly built shopping centre. His brash marketing and low prices would quickly capture the imagination of local customers. The landlords loved him – he helped to launch their developments so they helped him with his rent.

Although he didn't open his first proper shop until 1931, by 1939 Jack had 100 stores. After the war he grew his company rapidly by buying competitors and introducing his high volume, low price technique. Among the chains he bought were Victor Value and Irwins. By 1960 Tesco were operating over 800 outlets.

Jack had two daughters. At a time when women seldom worked in a family business or entered the board room, it was fortunate that both daughters found husbands with a business brain. His elder daughter Irene married Hyman Kreitman, son of a ladies' shoe manufacturer who, after being persuaded to join Tesco, played an important part in pushing Jack Cohen into the world of self-service retailing. Jack had visited the USA in the 1930s and seen the development of out-of-town self-service shopping, but didn't see that it would work in the UK. However, following another visit after the war Hyman Kreitman changed Jack's mind. In 1949 Kreitman was responsible for opening the first self-service Tesco in St Albans and during the next year three more followed. A previously reluctant Jack Cohen was persuaded by some highly encouraging sales and profit figures to give his son-in-law the go ahead to convert more stores to self-service. So far the stores were still small, at a time when the trend, led by Sainsbury's, was towards much bigger out-of-town supermarkets.

Kreitman, who was appointed joint managing director alongside Cohen in 1957, played an important part when trading stamps were being introduced. Initially Tesco, wishing to avoid the cost of commission charged by the trading stamp companies, were keen to steer clear. But when their biggest competitor Fine Fare started giving away Sperry & Hutchinson's (S+H) Pink Stamps, in 1963, Tesco were quick to follow suit with an agreement with the Green Shield Stamp company. With stamps being offered at many petrol stations, most consumers became collectors and Tesco attracted a significant number of new customers, at a time when price cutting was prevented by the law relating to resale price maintenance.

There was a constant tension between Cohen, who was still keen to take over more chains of small shops, and Kreitman, who saw that the key to future success was to build large supermarkets. When Cohen ignored his son-in-law's strategy by bidding for Unwins, a 212-store chain in North-West England, Kreitman felt so frustrated he quit.

Kreitman handed over the chair to Jack's second son-in-law, Leslie Porter, who married daughter Shirley. Like Kreitman, Porter also had a testy time with his father-in-law but enjoyed the support of his managing director, Ian MacLaurin, and resisted the attempts of Jack Cohen, now the Company President, to stop moving Tesco upmarket. A sense of how things felt in the board room is given by Porter's comment on his father-in-law: 'We value him going out to visit branches but as far as the day-to-day business is concerned he merely comments. We meet every Monday morning and reckon to get through most of the agenda before he arrives.' Jack Cohen was 75 years old when Porter became chairman, but probably still wanted to do what he was doing at 45.

Porter came from a textile background and steered Tesco into gradually adding clothing into some of the stores. With Cohen's grip having less influence, Tesco was free to build larger out-of-town stores with petrol stations and introduce a more stable style of management, which was perfect for Porter's successor Ian MacLaurin, who was the first non-family member to take charge of Tesco.

Ian MacLaurin

Ian MacLaurin is said to be Tesco's first management trainee, starting in 1959 at the age of 22. Life on the shop floor of a very down market grocer must have been a sharp contrast to his education at Malvern College. But, like previous Tesco leaders, he benefited from starting at the bottom as a butcher and warehouse assistant and never forgot his first management experience as a shop manager in Neasden.

When he was appointed Managing Director in 1973 MacLaurin inherited 1,000 stores, most of which had been bought in a series of deals with Tesco replacing the previous fascia, but still sitting in the same spot on the high street with the low-grade appeal of Cohen's 'Pile it high, sell it cheap'.

Meanwhile Sainsbury's was pulling in market share by opening out-of-town supermarkets and giving customers convenience, quality, value and a touch of snob appeal.

The catalyst for change came in one dramatic weekend, that of the Queen's Silver Jubilee in 1977, when MacLaurin scrapped the Green Shield Stamps, launched an aggressive price campaign called 'Operation Checkout' and announced his plan to close half the Tesco high street shops and replace them with loads more selling space out of town.

Literally overnight, MacLaurin said goodbye to Cohen's old Tesco and fired a gun that started 35 years of continuous growth.

Cohen had created a big business by extending his skills as a market trader. While keeping a reputation for keen prices, MacLaurin gave Tesco a strategy based on a customer-focused culture.

All the growth was now out of town. Instead of picking up more failing grocery companies Tesco took over some significant supermarket chains like Hillards with 40 stores in the North-East, and spent £640m buying the William Low supermarkets in Scotland, which Tesco won after a takeover battle with Sainsbury's, who were hoping to consolidate their market leadership by a major move north of the border.

Although MacLaurin achieved some growth by acquisition, to fulfil his plan to take Tesco totally out of town he needed to build new stores on green field sites. It was a challenge to convince the planners that the cheap, cheerful, but scruffy image

Tesco had presented in the past wouldn't be repeated in these new superstores. MacLaurin got his message across and when during the depressed trading of 1991/2 his competitors put expansion on hold, he went on a buying spree and built up a substantial land bank that was to feed Tesco's growth for more than a decade.

He recognised that Tesco's high levels of labour turnover were a sign of poor people policies, and embarked on a crusade to put people first, both employees and customers. It was an obvious strategy but one that many big retail groups ignore. While being wrapped up in meetings about shop design, pricing, TV advertising and store layout they forgot to think about their customers. Although some say retailing is all about location, location and location, even the best sited shops do much better if they are run by happy people with personality who are keen to look after the customers.

MacLaurin found a number of simple ways to give customers a better deal, but first he listened to what they had to say. As a result, to please mums, confectionery displays were removed from the checkouts to take temptation away from kids. To please everyone, more checkouts were manned if three people were waiting and, to give the personal touch, branch staff were encouraged to help customers asking for directions by walking with them to the product required. The whole theme of MacLaurin's approach was to be firmly on the customers' side, and to emphasise the approach, in 1992, the tag line 'Every little helps' was introduced.

MacLaurin was on a roll and took most of the Tesco employees along with him. Suddenly, instead of being simply shelf stackers and checkout operators, Tesco staff were in the customer care business. With a mission to provide a proper service and sales increasing, morale went up and Tesco store staff started to smile.

MacLaurin made another move, designed to get closer to his customers, when he tested the Tesco Clubcard in 1994. David Sainsbury ridiculed the scheme, suggesting it was no more than an electronic Green Shield Stamp, but the Clubcard brought Tesco much more than customer loyalty; they could now track what and when everyone was buying. Sainsbury's introduced their own Reward card three years later.

During Ian MacLaurin's time in charge at Tesco the company was transformed into a modern and efficient out-of-town superstore chain covering the UK and through the acquisition of the retail arm of Associated British Foods moved into Ireland. Before MacLaurin stepped down, Tesco overtook Sainsbury's as the market leader. In his 26 years as managing director and chairman he had created the most powerful culture and strategy in British retailing. But MacLaurin claimed that his greatest achievement was identifying Terry Leahy as his ideal successor.

Terry Leahy
Ian MacLaurin's blue-eyed boy passed the first critical test – he started at the bottom, stacking shelves. That was before he took a management degree at the University of Manchester Institute of Science and Technology (UMIST) where he was bound to have come under the influence of Professor Roland Smith, a blunt multi-company director, who I got to know when he masterminded the bust up in the Timpson board room that ended 107 years of family control. Leahy will have learnt about management by objectives with a macho touch, and if he had followed Smith's teaching he would have pursued a world of process and control rather than delegation.

Leahy may well have forgotten a lot of what he learnt at UMIST by the time he returned to Tesco in 1979 as a marketing executive at the age of 23. He joined the Board in 1992 and the part he played in developing Tesco's critical Clubcard must have helped him become chief executive in 1997.

Although some accounts give Leahy all the credit for the stunning success of Tesco under his leadership, it was MacLaurin who set the basic strategy that provided the platform for Leahy to develop. As soon as he took control, Leahy put his foot hard down on the accelerator and during his leadership Tesco ran fast in lots of directions.

Under MacLaurin, Tesco had already overtaken Sainsbury's as the market leader, but Leahy left their closest rival well behind by increasing the Tesco market share from 20 per cent to 30 per cent. Leahy soon realised there was a limit to the growth available through selling food in UK supermarkets and found ways to extend the Tesco brand into clothing, books, toys, electrical goods and photo processing.

Leahy modernised so much of Tesco it is surprising that he continued to run the business from such an unimpressive, random selection of offices as those which housed their headquarters in Cheshunt. Visitors who arrived expecting a modern reception area in an iconic building were in for a big disappointment.

Despite this lack of architectural style the Tesco management were a class act, with Leahy its dominant and respected leader, living the customer-based culture by visiting stores every Friday.

Everything Leahy and Tesco tackled seemed to turn into a success; if there was a weakness it was due to a touch of arrogance that was particularly resented by downtrodden suppliers and local communities who felt that the Tesco footprint was being stamped all over their back yard. Tesco got bigger by giving customers what they wanted, but then they discovered that being really big isn't in itself very popular. However, to Leahy, the battles he had to fight with local councils and communities, and the backlash from suppliers who claimed they were being bullied, seemed a small price to pay for the company's enormous success.

With such a big share of the UK market it wasn't surprising that Leahy became so keen on growing overseas. Starting in 1996, Tesco was welcomed in Budapest and Bangkok and the company built successful businesses in Poland, the Czech Republic, Slovakia, China, Malaysia, India and Turkey, and in 2006 couldn't resist the temptation to enter the USA with a start-up chain called Fresh & Easy.

Under Leahy, Tesco spotted the increasing demand for local shopping in convenience stores and as well as opening downtown Tesco Metro and Tesco Express, often linked to petrol stations, over 700 outlets were added with the acquisition in 2003 of One Stop, which still trades under the original name – few people realise it is yet another part of Tesco.

Leahy saw the Tesco future under four headings – UK, non-food, abroad and technical services. The Tesco brand was so strong it could make sure that every little helps for just about everything everyone needs. The Tesco Bank took them into financial services and the launch of tesco.com in 2000 led the home delivery field with Tesco Direct. Wherever you looked you saw Tesco success as turnover margins and profit grew every year under Leahy's leadership. When he stepped down to universal praise there was no suggestion that Leahy had made any major mistakes, but almost immediately profits started to fall and within four years Tesco was facing a major crisis.

You can question whether the difficulties were created by Philip Clarke (Leahy's chosen successor) or suggest the troubles were already there and Clarke was given a hospital pass.

In the late 1980s the consultant who told me that Next would hit 'the wall' could have made the same forecast about Tesco. No company is perfect and years of uninterrupted growth are certain to come to an end. The conglomerates of the 1970s and 80s such as Sears Holdings, UDS Group, Burton, Storehouse and Hanson Trust all split up. Tesco is similar – a conglomerate of businesses collected under the same brand. Rather than these businesses becoming too big to fail there were signs that they were too big to manage. The Tesco team didn't realise the complications until things started to go wrong. Every businessman has been told to keep it simple, but as the Leahy years went on Tesco got progressively more complicated. Although it has to be said that it was a fantastic achievement to make Tesco the brand that did almost all things for all men, in the end the hand that Leahy passed over to Clarke was certainly a pretty difficult one to play.

Perhaps Leahy was deceived by his own success. I am not convinced that management is a transferable skill; being really good at running food supermarkets doesn't mean you can run a bank.

Cheshunt might not look great from the outside, but together with the offices down the road at Welwyn Garden City they housed a lot of Tesco managers, probably too many. Parkinson (of Parkinson's Law) was right: as organisations grow they develop more levels of management than they need. Tesco certainly did. A surplus of middle management encourages company politics and the development of processes designed to tell customer-facing colleagues what to do. Leahy had the loyalty of lots of talented executives but it isn't surprising, with so many fighting each other for the next big job, many left Tesco to claim top jobs elsewhere. Economic commentators were quick to point out that the supermarket problems of 2014 were mainly due to the competition from Aldi, Lidl and Waitrose, made worse by there being too many supermarkets with too much space in a period when food prices were going down. Leahy must have spotted the change in shopping behaviour many years earlier, when he developed Tesco Express, opened more Tesco Metros and bought One Stop. But despite seeing the appeal of convenience stores, the Tesco Extra supermarket development programme that began in 1997 continued. Perhaps Leahy was keen to outgun the other chains by opening more new shops, especially as he had a massive land bank to fuel the expansion.

Despite the help of market research studies into each catchment area, spreadsheets showing spending potential by socio-economic group, and the wealth of information provided by the Tesco Clubcard, many of the new units fell well short of expectations. Some shoppers didn't like the bigger shops with their ground level car parks and escalators to the trading floor, which gave over half the space to non-food merchandise. These new megastores were a sign that Tesco was getting too big for anyone's good. Every little might help, but getting even bigger wasn't popular.

Leahy's routine Friday branch visits couldn't keep him in total touch with a business that extended from Chiswick to China and was selling everything from tomatoes to trousers and lupins to laptops. It is very difficult to maintain a strong company culture when you have 350,000 employees. With the Tesco culture getting weaker and more branch colleagues joining the shop workers' union, things changed. Today's Tesco employs too many people who never seem to smile and simply need a job. I feel sorry for the superstars who have been swamped in the Tesco drive to get bigger.

No doubt Philip Clarke was delighted that Terry Leahy picked him out as his successor but he was probably given an impossible task. Some say it would have helped if Clarke had possessed more charisma. He might have been too hasty to part company with most of his senior colleagues who had been his fellow travellers in the Leahy years but he clearly inherited a lot of problems for which Leahy himself had no solution.

Clarke started on the right path by closing Fresh & Easy in the US, but it quickly became clear that the biggest problem, by far, was weak figures from the core supermarket business in the UK. When companies diversify it is important to continue to produce good results from the core business.

Philip Clarke lasted less than four years and left the company before he could produce a viable plan. It is now up to his successor, Dave Lewis, who will have less time to come up with a solution.

Tesco still has a great customer base and a fantastic history but it got too complicated. The days of Tesco getting bigger have probably come to an end. The business needs to be simpler to run, which may require saying goodbye to many of the areas developed by Terry Leahy – it could be that by becoming smaller Tesco will get stronger. Every little helps!

SAINSBURY'S

In about 1969 I went to Sainsbury's head office, which was then south of the Thames, to find out more about the Sainsbury computer system because they were leading the field in retail stock control by computer. I don't remember much about the technology but I will never forget their culture. In a word they were arrogant. Within minutes I felt less than two feet tall, a Northern footwear retailer who was a million miles behind this smart London-based supermarket group that was showing every other shopkeeper how to do business. They might have appeared haughty and offhand, but they had a fair amount to be arrogant about.

Their family business was started five years after Timpson but we'd floated in 1929 and were now about to lose control while the Sainsbury family still owned 100 per cent of a company that made twenty times as much money.

Romantically, the first shop was opened in 1869 in Drury Lane, London by John James Sainsbury, whose first job was in a grocery shop, and his fiancée Mary Ann, whose father had a small chain of dairy shops in North London. The shop, which mainly sold eggs, butter and milk, opened when they got married and two years later they lived above their second shop in Kentish Town, where they soon opened two more shops close by. Their success was based on providing top quality with fantastic value, and it worked so well they were able to set up shop in Croydon, an upmarket move that set the scene for Sainsbury's future appeal to the more affluent consumers who are looking for great value.

Most of the growth was concentrated in London, where it was possible to open outlets within a few hundred yards of each other – most people walked to the shops, but Sainsbury's gave them the cherished benefit of home delivery. By 1925, 56 years after the first shop and three years before John James Sainsbury died, the company had 166 shops as far afield as Norwich, Oxford, Bournemouth and Cambridge.

The Sainsbury family was lucky to have a succession of able entrepreneurs with the ability to keep their extended family shareholders on side and the talent to continue to grow their family business.

The founder was succeeded by his son John Benjamin Sainsbury, who continued to follow the principles laid down by his parents and in 1938 handed over control to his sons Alan and Robert who started an initiative that put Sainsbury's ahead of all their competitors.

In the late 1940s there was considerable speculation about the self-service shops that were becoming a significant part of food retailing in the USA. Most UK travellers who spotted the new way of shopping thought up all the reasons why it wouldn't happen in the UK, including: we don't rely as much on the car, our customers are faithful to their local shop, and we don't always follow what happens in America.

In 1950 Sainsbury's started to convert well-established shops to self-service, and the family management team went further; they had the courage to open bigger and bigger new self-service food shops, more and more out of town. Sainsbury's were in the forefront of the supermarket revolution, while others stood by waiting for Sainsbury's to trip up.

It was the perfect time for the most talented member of the Sainsbury dynasty, the 42-year-old John Davan Sainsbury, to take charge at the top of his family company.

John Davan Sainsbury

In 1969 John Davan (JD) took over as chief executive from the successful partnership of his uncle Robert, who was the finance expert, and his father Alan, the trader. Alan provided JD with his formula for success based on the development of self-service with the promise that 'good food costs less at Sainsbury's'.

JD, who followed his education at Stowe and Oxford with experience in several Sainsbury's departments, including many years as a buyer, dominated the company during his 23 years as executive chairman. He was the face of Sainsbury's, always pictured in a store, leading from the front. When he took over the chairmanship, Tesco were making double the profit of Sainsbury's, a fact that must have severely irritated the Sainsburys' pride. The nice family business that appealed to middle-income London families was being beaten by a barrow-boy-based brand from the East End.

Perhaps it was the pursuit of Tesco, or more likely it was family pride that made JD such a driven boss. His father had provided the success formula but JD was ruthless in putting it into practice.

In 1969 there were still 82 out of 244 shops offering a counter service. JD didn't just convert them to self-service, he replaced them with much bigger out-of-town supermarkets. In ten years he only grew the business to 300 stores but an average outlet was now over four times the size with twenty times the trade. When JD floated Sainsbury's on the Stock Market in 1973 the market capitalisation was £117m. By the time he retired as chairman it was worth £8.1bn and Sainsbury's was about to regain the crown as market leader by overtaking Tesco.

All the figures suggest that JD was an unqualified success, but some say he was a somewhat short-tempered autocrat who expected every employee to follow the letter of the company rules and ran the stores with an incredible attention to detail.

Like me, he believed in the importance of regular branch visits, wanting to see the business from a customer's point of view by turning up at stores without any prior warning. The style and purpose of our visits, however, were totally different. I travel round to meet our colleagues, listen to what they say and hope to pick up some new ideas. JD on the other hand expected perfection and was on the lookout for any part of the store that was below standard. Store employees must have dreaded his sudden and unpredictable appearances and would surely have been mightily relieved if he left without spotting a major problem.

He might have been a short-tempered nit-picker but he certainly knew what he wanted and knew the business. He achieved so much that it is churlish to suggest he could have done so much more if he had been able to delegate. It must have been particularly frustrating for the buyers who had to submit all new packaging to JD for his personal approval.

JD was so single-minded and sure of himself he was unimpressed by the move into non-food merchandise at Tesco and Asda (which he dismissed as being a Northern-based business). When he did decide to widen the offer he did it in partnership with British Home Stores (BHS) in a number of stores branded SavaCentre.

These big stores, which were JD's answer to the big Carrefour, Asda and Tesco hypermarkets, were all connected to newly built shopping centres; the first SavaCentre was linked to The Galleries in Washington and opened in 1977. I first spotted a SavaCentre in Hempstead Valley, the second location for this new format, and thought that Sainsbury's and BHS were strange bedfellows. The opening programme had reached fewer than twenty stores in 1989 when Sainsbury's bought out the BHS stake (by now owned by Storehouse). JD seemed to like joint ventures (somewhat surprising for someone so dictatorial). He linked with Belgian retailer GB-Inno-BM to create Homebase, which was designed to bring a supermarket approach to the DIY market. Although many of the original Homebase sites were next door to Sainsbury's stores they never felt part of the Sainsbury's offer. Homebase got a lot bigger after the purchase of Texas Homecare in 1995 and the chain provided a welcome source of cash when it was sold to venture capitalist Schroder Ventures in 2000 for £750m, with a further £219m coming from the sale of 28 development sites to Kingfisher's B&Q. Although it always seemed a strange development for Sainsbury's, JD's venture into the DIY business created quite a lot of cash.

JD's other big deal took Sainsbury's into the USA with the purchase of Shaw's Supermarket. The move was totally out of character; why would someone with such a love for detail and complete control want to invest a lot of money on the other side of the Atlantic? The desire to repeat UK success abroad, especially in the USA, seldom seems to work and in most cases is as inexplicable as shrewd entrepreneurs investing their money in a football club. The Shaw's saga didn't work out too badly for Sainsbury's. Although the business must have caused them a lot of hassle and soaked up plenty of time, it was eventually sold in 2004 for £2.48bn.

JD's time as chairman put Sainsbury's on top of the UK supermarket league and with its theme that good food costs less at Sainsbury's they became the place of choice for middle-class shoppers, especially in the South-East of England. Under JD, Sainsbury's was perhaps even more arrogant, but they had even more to be arrogant about.

From David Sainsbury to Peter Davis

After four generations of inspirational leaders Sainsbury's was suddenly running out of Sainsburys who were both willing and able to do the job. JD was succeeded by his cousin David who, it is said, only joined the family business in the personnel department when he couldn't pursue his preferred career as a scientist. David was on the Sainsbury's board for 25 years, so he certainly knew a lot about the business that was run by cousin John, but companies don't just need chairmen who can follow in their predecessor's footsteps; each generation must bring their own individual sparkle and breathe brand-new life into the culture. JD had set out with a mission to overtake Tesco, maximise self-service, grow out of town and continue to follow in his predecessors' footsteps by providing 'the best butter for less'. He seldom bothered about the competitors; JD did things his way.

David Sainsbury was far more placid, he preferred consensus to confrontation and was happy to go along with the flow rather than make things happen. Without a simple driving strategy it wasn't surprising that things started to go wrong – poorly run businesses seem to get more than their fair share of bad luck.

David would have had more chance of success if he hadn't lost two of JD's most experienced henchmen. In 1994 sales fell – something hitherto unknown at Sainsbury's – and the 'Essentials for Essentials' price-cutting campaign was considered a failure, so buying director and deputy chairman Tom Vyner got the blame and eventually left the company. His senior colleague David Quarmby, their logistics guru, had already left after Dino Adriano had been promoted over his head in a management reshuffle. David Sainsbury had a habit of fudging appointments and was strongly criticised when Adriano was appointed as a joint chief executive alongside David Bremner, who was responsible for Homebase and overseas.

All this deck-chair moving in the board room wouldn't have mattered if Sainsbury had championed a forward thinking strategy, but most of the time was spent playing catch-up.

David Sainsbury derided the Tesco Clubcard but eighteen months later introduced his own Reward card (later converted to Nectar). Sainsbury's were slow to follow Tesco and Asda into the non-food market. When Tesco started to open convenience stores with Tesco Express, Sainsbury's followed with Sainsbury's Local. At every turn Sainsbury's were being beaten to the punch. Sainsbury's suffered a big psychological blow when they lost to Tesco in the bidding war for William Low Supermarkets in Scotland and morale sank even lower when Tesco took over as market leader. They were even losing their reputation for quality to M&S and Waitrose.

David Sainsbury was succeeded as chairman by George Bull, the first non-family member to take the chair. By that time Dino Adriano was sole chief executive but, after an unwise appearance on a fly-on-the-wall documentary, Bull replaced him with Peter Davis who had been at Sainsbury's during the JD days.

Peter Davis had a plan – his 'Business Transformation Programme' – which was more about logistics than strategy or culture. His main aim was to cure the current stock availability problems by investing £3bn in store layout, IT and distribution, including four state-of-the-art warehouses at £100m each.

Although Davis was a popular choice with the City, prospects still hadn't improved when after nearly four years as chief executive Davis passed on the challenge to Justin King.

Justin King

Justin King was the perfect choice to put Sainsbury's back on track. He came in March 2004 from M&S where he was responsible for food; previously he had worked at Asda with Archie Norman and Allan Leighton, which is almost certainly where he learnt how to understand both customers and colleagues.

He joined a business that had a reputation for high prices, empty shelves and disillusioned staff. Sales at Sainsbury's were not only well behind Tesco, they had even been overtaken by Asda. He took his time, keen to get to know the business before taking action or making promises, but he was quick to seek the consumer view: 250,000 customers responded to his questionnaire, and King used their opinions to put together his plan, labelled 'Making Sainsbury's Great Again'.

He found an expert to fix his supply chain, which meant mending the damage done by Peter Davis's hasty investment in four warehouses which suffered from serial system failures. The rest of the King recovery was based on plenty of listening and a lot of common sense.

King didn't find the answer by sitting in a lot of meetings, commissioning vital market research or calling in a consultant. The secret was to take note of customers' comments and talk to the colleagues who talked to customers. Like JD, King spent a fair amount of time in the stores, but unlike JD he was one of the team, wearing a Sainsbury's badge and happy to serve customers.

Early on he shifted the balance of power by reducing the head office payroll by 750 people and employing 3,000 more out in the field. He showed his faith in himself and the future by announcing an ambitious sales target, aiming to increase turnover by £2.5bn within four years and he had the confidence to halve the dividend to help finance his plan. Shareholders, especially the Sainsbury family, would expect him to deliver on his promise.

King was keen to match Tesco in the move towards more convenience stores and in his first year in post acquired the 54-store Bells chain in North-East England, and Jacksons based in Yorkshire that had 114 stores. During the same year, some welcome cash came from the sale of Shaw's Supermarkets in the USA.

King easily delivered his promised growth in sales and continued to show increases for the next ten years, recording his first fall six months before stepping down in 2014.

King didn't do anything clever but he was smart. His time at Asda taught him the benefits of talking to colleagues on every level in a way that treated them as equals. He was smart to use the phrase 'Making Sainsbury's Great Again' because it described his campaign to capture the old values in a modern context. But he didn't bring back the old Sainsbury's arrogance. His style was to be a down-to-earth retailer who led from the shop floor. True, whenever he was caught on camera, usually visiting a store, he always looked pretty pleased with himself, but it is fair to say that he had plenty to be pleased about.

It is said of politicians that their career is almost bound to end in failure. Chief executives, whatever they achieve while in post, are often criticised for their legacy – or in some cases the mess they leave for others to clear up. King stepped down at a relatively young age and some could cruelly say that his timing was within six months of being perfect. But you can't blame him for leaving early enough to have a crack at another big job before retirement. He left at a tricky time for the sector and Mike Coupe, his successor, has a difficult task, but King handed over a much fitter business than he inherited.

ASDA

Archie Norman and Allan Leighton

Most retail chains are started in one shop by one person with the entrepreneurial flair and ambition to build a bigger business. Asda was different: it had its origins in the 1920s when a group of Yorkshire dairy farmers joined forces to develop outlets for their products and diversify into the world of retailing. In 1965, as Associated Dairies and Farm Stores Ltd, they merged with Asquith's, a small chain of supermarkets, and became Asda, formed from the first two letters of each name. The venture worked quite well, but Asda stores were pretty much the same as their main competitors until, in the same year, they acquired a company called GEM which owned two stores, one in Leeds, the other near Nottingham at West Bridgford. The Nottingham store was huge and due to its poor trading GEM had lost so much money the Asda team was able to buy it for nothing ... and they had a plan.

With a combination of food at fantastic value and a big

range of non-food supplied by franchisees the Asda team filled the 70,000-square-foot store, increased sales to over £40,000 a week and found a success formula that set them apart from any other retailer.

The big store offering low-price food alongside a comprehensive collection of clothing, homeware, white goods and anything else you could think of was a fantastic formula for Asda to exploit. As they started to spread the concept to converted mills and large green field sites it was clear they had stolen a march on the rest of the food retailers who were just getting their mind around 20,000-square-foot stores.

In the late 1970s and early 80s when Asda needed to keep things simple they made life complicated. To secure sites for future development they bought existing sheds from the furniture trade and fell in love with them. Instead of building a lot more big Asda stores they devoted time to the furniture shops, which traded as Allied Carpets and Wades Furniture. They also negotiated a merger with MFI which didn't last long, but at least when Asda–MFI split up, the Asda team was no longer distracted by the frustrations of selling furniture.

Sales and profits started to climb after John Fletcher (ex-Harvard and Warburton's the bakers) was drafted in as chief executive. John was a personable and ambitious entrepreneur, as I discovered when we chatted during several afternoons on the boundary and the touch line watching our sons playing on the same school teams. It was also clear that John was his own man, with a strong feeling of self-belief. He continued to open more stores but deviated from the Asda blueprint by pushing up margins and keeping clear of own brands. Initially profits increased but when Asda started to struggle as competitors gained ground by selling more quality own brands at great value, Fletcher was asked to leave and the top job was taken on by John Hardman, who Fletcher had brought in as Financial Director.

Hardman tried to reverse the mistakes by introducing an own label, tightening margins and opening more shops, especially in the South of England. To accelerate the growth he bought 60 of the biggest stores from Gateway for £700m. He was investing too much and growing too fast in too many directions at once. The business had totally lost its way when Archie Norman was brought in from his job as Group FD at Kingfisher in the hope that he could work a miracle.

Norman cleverly lowered City expectations to give himself more breathing space and, having done the usual tour round the business and called in a few consultants, Norman worked out his strategy for survival, which included the recruitment of Allan Leighton, a marketing man from Mars UK, as his right-hand man.

To me it doesn't matter whether you give the major credit to Archie Norman or Allan Leighton; between them they not only turned round a very sick business but in the process created one of the strongest company cultures in the country.

Their game plan included the usual cull at head office and a thorough overhaul of the merchandise with a special recognition of the need to overcome a woeful reputation for fresh quality produce. They did all the things an accomplished multiple retailer would do but they did something more that put the buzz into Asda stores.

The defining moment was when Leighton declared that he wanted to be in a business that put colleagues and customers first. He accepted Asda had to give value, especially as a lot of the stores were in low-income areas of the country. But to him just because the produce was lower in price didn't mean the customers should have to put up with poor quality or poor service. His big mission was to look after the colleagues who delivered the service. Norman and Leighton had the vision of cheap but very cheerful stores staffed by smiling colleagues who were happy to work for a fairly wacky style of management. With Asda attracting more than its fair share of young customers it helped to be unconventional and stand out from the stuffy Sainsbury's stores and tacky Tesco.

A lot of the showbiz approach was imported from the USA where Leighton clearly loved the extrovert style of American shopping, especially at Walmart. From the greeter at the front of the store with an enormous name badge, to the superior facilities in the staff room, everything possible was done to emphasise the importance of customers and colleagues.

I have found Asda to be a fantastic hunting ground for new ideas. We still use their technique of having one Perfect Day every year when every shop and every colleague is expected to be perfect (it is the one way we have found that can really lift standards throughout the business). Another popular Asda import is the home-produced scratch cards that managers hand out to recognise high performers and unsung heroes (ours carry prizes that include £50, a meal out for two, and 'the next sale is yours'). Our most effective Asda idea is the regular Town Hall meeting that James holds at least every month to update everyone in our offices.

Asda have had the courage to be really different with a loud, eccentric greeter at the entrance to their Leeds head office and a colleague huddle before the store opens to talk through the day ahead. The huddle ends with the Asda chant: 'Give us an A ... Give us an S ... Give us a D ...' You can guess the rest.

The beauty of the Asda culture is that it covers all aspects of the business and is consistent. When Next shops first appeared it was said that every aspect of the new business, from shop fitting to merchandise, had been written by the same pair of hands. The same can be said of the Asda culture.

With such a clear sense of direction it was surprising that Asda, having said goodbye to carpets, were still tempted to do more deals. You can only wonder why they contemplated buying Roadchef and although there was more logic in buying Safeway they may have found it even more difficult to digest than Ken Morrison did 25 years later. The other deal that never happened was a possible merger with The Kingfisher Group, who in those days included Woolworths, B&Q, Superdrug and Comet. Before discussions could get serious Asda agreed to sell to Walmart and has stuck to the big supermarket formula ever since. The Walmart team can't have believed their luck when they discovered that their new acquisition had already adopted most of the best Walmart ideas and made them work brilliantly in Britain.

Archie Norman moved into politics and Allan Leighton declared he was going plural (as I find it impossible to do more than one thing at once I found it a strange concept). But the culture they established at Asda was so strong it continued under their successors Tony de Nuncio, Andy Bond and Andy Clarke.

Archie Norman and Allan Leighton taught the rest of the retail world that shopkeeping is not just about location, location, location – it is much more about people: the colleagues and the customers.

MORRISONS

Ken Morrison

Just like the newly married Sainsburys 30 years earlier, Ken Morrison's father started in business in 1899 selling butter and eggs. But there was a big difference between the Sainsbury's shop in Drury Lane, London and Morrison's market stall in Bradford. The North–South divide is well expressed by the difference in character between Morrisons and Sainsbury's.

Ken was involved in the business from an early age; it is even suggested that he was behind the counter at the age of five and was regularly serving customers in his school holidays. In 1952 when his father fell ill, Ken, then in his mid-twenties and just returned from national service, took over the management of the small chain of stalls and shops.

Within two years he opened his first self-service shop with three checkouts and two years later developed a 5,000-square-foot supermarket. The business grew rapidly in Yorkshire and crossed the Pennines when Ken bought Whelan Discount from ex-footballer Dave Whelan, who went on to set up JJB Sports. By 1999 Ken had a chain of 100 stores.

Ken Morrison learnt from experience and knew what he wanted. He developed the business his way for the Yorkshire customer and wasn't much bothered what anyone else thought or what everyone else did. Ken came from the business school of common sense with little time for statistics and IT. He certainly would never have used consultants and their research into catchment areas and socio-economic groups to tell him where to open the next shop. He claims his technique was to 'get on a bus and look for chimneys'. Likewise Ken was dismissive of the City, analysts and journalists. When institutional shareholders were insisting that he appoint non-executive directors he pointed out that he could get two more good checkout girls for the same money. His competitors, who copied many of his ideas, recognised that Ken was the cleverest in the business, but his hands-on approach mystified the smart young open-shirted MBA marketing and strategy experts who couldn't understand how Ken could run his business by instinct rather than a statistically based master plan. Too few understood the Northern-based culture or travelled to Yorkshire to find out.

Morrisons supermarkets with their distinctive Market Street were a development of Ken's imagination. He knew his business by being in the stores and, it is rumoured, rooting in bins to see if any saleable goods were being wasted or tearing open sandwich packets to check if they were fresh. He was so close to his customers he talked to some of them almost every day and realised the prime importance of providing fresh quality products at great value. To secure the right supplies, he pursued a policy of vertical integration going back as far as food processing and farming.

Ken clearly led from the front. His character was stamped all over the stores and, unlike most big businesses, a Morrisons colleague on the shop floor would probably know their boss. It helps morale and respect when junior employees can meet the owner.

All went well until Ken agreed to bid for Safeway in December 2003. I remember visiting a Safeway store a few weeks after the bid and it looked as if it was closing down – lacking buzz and short of stock, surrounded by staff who were expecting redundancy. Within weeks the breakdown in stock distribution to Safeway shops had caused such chaos even some of the most loyal customers were turned off for good.

Having taken over many competitors I recognised the

symptoms. It takes a long time to get the newly acquired employees on your side. They will expect the new management to be at least as bad as the last lot and reserve judgement until given a good reason to trust the new boss. It is wise to let normal business continue as long as possible so you can get to know as much as you can about the new business before making major changes. With Safeway, there was the added North/South problem. Colleagues and customers connected to the southern Safeway stores resented the idea of having a Yorkshire culture thrust upon them. Before they tried to learn about the way Morrison ticks they had already decided it wasn't for them.

Nearly every takeover brings a traumatic digestion period when profits can fall and management struggle to keep the core business going while making loads of little decisions on the new toy. After every acquisition I have discovered some new surprises. Morrisons were bound to be in for a few shocks after their first major acquisition which involved over 550 stores. There is little doubt that Ken's retail magic would work just as well in Kingston as Keighley but it had to be introduced carefully. It wasn't.

At the first sign of weakness the smart City analysts took the chance to criticise Ken, the maverick who they considered to be out of his depth. They claimed that you couldn't run a business without putting proper processes in place; no one should run a modern business simply by flair and common sense.

Safeway stores recovered but Sir Ken Morrison didn't. In retrospect it is amazing that he survived so long using such an individual approach to run a public company. The fact that he ran the business for 50 years and retired as chairman with profits of over £600m from about 550 stores shows quite clearly that you can run a company by relying on common sense, especially if you have the rare talent of Ken Morrison.

MARKS & SPENCER

Marks & Spencer is named after the partnership of Michael Marks and Tom Spencer that was formed in the 1890s, but it was Marks' family and that of his son-in-law, Michael Sieff, who turned the company into a national chain.

It is difficult to know where to put most credit among the Marks (Michael and Simon) and the Sieffs (Israel, Marcus and Edmund), but between them they did an amazing job between 1894 and 1984, building everything that made Marks & Spencer an example for the rest of us to follow. It can't have been part of a long-term plan; no one could have foreseen how a market stall in Leeds, followed by a Penny Bazaar in Birkenhead and their first proper shop in Cheetham Hill, north of Manchester city centre would blossom into the chain that dominated our high streets after the Second World War.

As a fellow retailer I confess to feeling, at the time, a slight irritation at the unique reputation their stores had in the eyes of customers, which implied, perhaps rightly, that all other multiple chains were in another, inferior, league. This jealousy didn't stop me admiring their achievements and trying to copy some of their best ideas. There is no doubt that the Marks and the Sieffs developed a business and created a culture that showed how, by running a really good business, you also make very good money.

The M&S culture based on quality, value, integrity, and high standards meant that every part of the business followed the same philosophy. Customers, colleagues and suppliers all enjoyed the benefits of being part of the M&S experience. Customers got a fair deal, especially if they had a problem. The M&S no-quibble returns policy, which allowed exchange or a refund on any recent purchase, may have encouraged some unscrupulous customers to claim money for slightly worn or even shoplifted garments but the cost was well worth the reputation earned for great customer care, which was reflected in all the other ways customers were treated. Although M&S was mostly self-service, pleasant staff were usually willing to give a helping hand.

The stores weren't spectacular but they were spotless. M&S was always happier to be a follower of fashion than a leader and the store design provided a comfortable welcome for most age groups. Teenagers found little of interest in M&S but returned as regular customers as soon as the first baby was born. For a lot of basic purchases most people recognised that M&S was the most obvious, easiest and best place to shop.

The promise of 100 per cent British goods was an important cornerstone of the M&S image. It was a way of underlining their quality while reassuring regular customers that they were being loyal to home-based industry. At a time when cheaper, often shoddy, imports were starting to threaten UK manufacturers, the 'British only' claim gave M&S a special place on the moral high ground.

Support for home produce meant they had to develop a special way to work with suppliers which went well beyond the usual buyer/seller relationship. Many regarded selection as an M&S supplier to be a major accolade, a sign that the supplier was well run and had high quality standards. Such recognition generally came with the promise of a long order book and support from M&S research and development. But M&S suppliers had to maintain high standards to keep their membership of this exclusive club. The rigorous inspections by quality control and the expectations of good housekeeping, prompt deliveries and exclusivity meant many suppliers had to sell their soul to M&S to keep the business.

Customers came to rely on M&S quality and some items like socks and knickers were so popular they achieved enormous shares of the market. By working so closely with manufacturers M&S was able to develop whole ranges of merchandise that enjoyed special customer appeal and a commanding position in the market. Men's suits and women's cashmere sweaters were examples of the M&S master touch.

The best example of the M&S ability to innovate and create a new market was, and still is, in food. They were at the forefront of developing convenience food, introducing sell-by dates in 1970 and tempting a large number of British households to try things like avocado, fresh orange juice and prawn cocktail in a way that persuaded people to pay premium prices for good quality produce. Customers were happy to foot the bill for quality they could trust because it came with the M&S values.

To underpin the whole philosophy, M&S was able to attract great employees. No other retailer did so much to pamper their shop workers. From 1930 onwards a new improved staff welfare policy began to develop such benefits as cut-price chiropody and hairdressing, free health screening for breast and cervical cancer, healthy food in the canteen and a free uniform, with the girls getting a generous supply of American tan coloured tights. It wasn't surprising that so many people applied to work for M&S; the company could take their pick from the best available talent. This was particularly true of management trainees, who were given an all-round grounding in retailing from shop floor to the buying departments. M&S management training was a passport to lots of the top jobs throughout retailing.

In the mid-1980s M&S seemed to have it all. Years of dedicated development based on a social conscience and a passion for excellence had created a complete culture that set the chain apart from all those that claimed to be competitors. But the next few years showed that it was not so easy to keep those traditions up to date.

Perhaps someone should have written down the things that made the difference, a list of the essential building blocks that made M&S such a powerful force. It would have included at its core the way they looked after their colleagues and customers and how they valued suppliers. But even with these core values the company still needs to be led by someone with the flair to fashion the culture from decade to decade. Things seem to have slipped as soon as Marcus Sieff stepped down as skipper in 1984.

M&S had become the UK's most profitable retailer but I suspect this was achieved more by aiming to be a great business rather than by purely planning for a great profit. The first non-family chairmen Derek Reyner and Richard Greenbury were keen to take the company to £1bn profit, which they did in 1998, but perhaps in doing so they sacrificed some of the principles that underpinned the stores' previous success.

It is difficult for managers who take on the management of such a big successful business. They have to make progress, shareholders want bigger dividends and higher profits to make the share price rise, while colleagues need a new challenge – no one wants to work for a declining or stagnant company. But with the awesome success M&S had achieved, it was difficult to get even bigger and keep the culture.

Taking M&S overseas was never going to be easy. The strong ethos of 'Made in Britain' was bound to have a mixed reception in Paris, and the functional layout of the stores that sits so well on an English shopping street looked desperately drab when I went to an M&S in Toronto (although they did rescue me from the embarrassment of forgetting to pack any shirts!). The purchase of Brooks Brothers in the USA defies any logic – M&S was simply not equipped to run a different sort of company in a completely different country. By looking for growth overseas the directors were using up precious time, cash, thought and energy that should have been used developing, updating and growing the core business.

By first straining every muscle and squeezing every cost centre to reach £1bn profit and then trying to satisfy the City by recovering from a profits collapse, successive M&S boards have abandoned many of the basic pillars of the company culture and, in the absence of flair they relied on best practice and process to deliver some decent short-term figures to the City.

The Buy British policy disappeared in the 1990s with the general collapse of the UK's manufacturing base, but even with the freedom to source from around the world M&S found it hard to compete with Primark, Next, and New Look.

Due to a touch of arrogance and a lack of judgement M&S refused to accept Visa or MasterCard payments until 2000, 34 years after credit cards first became part of the retail world. This reluctance to accept the most popular forms of payment was an early sign that management had stopped talking to their customers and perhaps were spending too much time in meetings and not enough talking to colleagues in the stores. A succession of chairmen and chief executives struggled to find the formula to put M&S back on track. Luc Vandevelde, Roger Holmes, Stuart Rose and most recently Marc Boland all made progress in sections of the business but none recaptured the sparkle which lit up our high streets under the guidance of the Marks and the Sieffs. In the 1990s and 2000s the company tried to extend the brand to everything from bedding to banking. They did a brilliant job on food but lost ground in the area that mattered most – women's fashion. They were, with the possible exception of the Per Una range, catering for an ageing population of loyal customers while their competitors had the styles to capture the next generation of shoppers.

M&S-bashing became a popular sport for financial journalists who, as they have done more recently with Tesco, encouraged shareholders to give the Board a hard time. Thankfully the City's displeasure was not enough to back Philip Green's bid in 2004. Stuart Rose did the high street a big favour by fighting off his rival. The poor performance of British Home Stores shows that Green, who was great at doing deals, probably did not have the expertise to put the magic back into M&S. The only possible predator equipped to put M&S back on its pedestal was, and is, Next plc.

The biggest difference in today's M&S is the look in the eye of customer-facing colleagues. They don't seem to feel special because the 'best in class' approach to recruitment, training and employee perks seems to have disappeared. At its worst moments the checkout queues were growing to W.H. Smith levels.

M&S is still a good business but it's no longer a great business. I still buy their basic suits and seldom go anywhere else for socks and underpants but I can't help feeling sorry for them, especially when they feel forced to put on a store-wide sale ten days before Christmas. The feeling is similar to watching a well-known football team that has been relegated from the Premier League.

I still prefer to think of M&S in the halcyon days when they were on top form and were the clear retail leader of the day. Many of the lessons we learnt from them then are still just as helpful today.

DRESS SHOPS AND FASHION

Shops and shopping have shifted significantly during the last 50 years and some of the most dramatic changes have been in the women's fashion sector.

In 1960 womenswear shops had big windows with little on show inside. There was no self-service and little opportunity to browse round the shop but there were plenty of sales assistants on hand, all working on commission.

The successful shops had the latest fashions in the window and the best sales staff inside. Companies founded in the 1920s were the well-established market and fashion leaders and customers were very happy to shop in a number of multiples like Dorothy Perkins, Etam, Wallis and Richard Shops.

Dorothy Perkins, with its little tiled roof over each window, became part of the Burton Group (now itself a subsidiary of the Arcadia Group). In 1979, Etam was swallowed up by Philip Green who distributed the shops between various Arcadia fascias in 2005. Wallis, well known for interpreting the latest Paris collections, became a subsidiary of Sears which also finished up in the hands of Philip Green. Richard Shops, probably the strongest fashion name of the 1960s, was guided by Rudy Weil who was seen as a true fashion leader. Founded in 1927, Richard Shops became part of United Drapery Stores (UDS) before being acquired by Terence Conran's Storehouse, which eventually sold the chain to Sears, which in turn ultimately became part of Philip Green's Arcadia Group in 1999.

So most of the main fashion shop names of the 1950s, 60s and 70s are now owned by Philip Green, and he bought most of them for next to nothing.

But in 1960 they were all doing pretty well, oblivious to the whirlwind that was waiting in the wings. Fashion was about to undergo a revolution, with a new wave of designers creating fashion for the mods and rockers. Teenagers started demanding different styling and new shops for their generation. Enter Carnaby Street, Biba, Mary Quant and Twiggy. A new order hit the high street.

Biba, an iconic store in Kensington, was created by Barbara Hulanicki, a Polish girl who studied at the Brighton School of Art before becoming a freelance fashion illustrator for publications including *Vogue* and *Tatler*.

After selling her first clothing designs through mail order she opened a shop in Kensington in 1964 and by 1969 Biba was established on Kensington High Street.

She didn't do any conventional shopfitting – Biba was designed to shock with Art Nouveau decor and elaborate props. Barbara's Biba provided the media with perfect copy, counting Mick Jagger, Marianne Faithfull and David Bowie among her customers. I went there as well and, although my visit didn't feature in the press, it did convince me to treble the order quantity of our copy of the Biba boot – a nearly thigh-high plain boot that the whole country wanted to buy. One shop in London was dictating fashion to the whole country.

Biba was born at the perfect time and Barbara Hulanicki was tuned in to the new world of miniskirts, floppy hats and T-shirts, but Biba didn't last long. Fashion moves in a cycle.

In my world of shoes it takes about twenty years for styles to go from pointed toes to big round toes and back to points. To maintain a long-term fashion business your style sense needs to move with the fashion cycle. But Biba didn't disappear just because it was trapped in a 60s rock and bohemian culture. Biba got too big too quickly. Most people give credit to the new kid on the block. When Biba's first shop appeared on Abingdon Road, customers enjoyed discovering the new place to shop, and when the store moved to Kensington Church Street the same loyal customers shared in the success. But the move to a bigger store on Kensington High Street meant that the loyal original customers were now sharing the Biba secret with a much wider audience.

When in 1974 Biba moved into the seven-storey Derry and Toms department store, it became too big at the very moment that fashion moved away from the magic of the 60s. The big Biba department store lasted little more than a year.

Biba didn't become a long-term business but Barbara Hulanicki's brainchild made a lasting impression on the high street.

*

In my role as a shoe buyer, as well as self-consciously visiting Biba I also paid regular visits to Carnaby Street, which also made an impression on the national fashion scene. I joined the crowds window-shopping stores with attitude and wonderful names, including 'Kleptomania' and 'I was Lord Kitchener's Valet', while keeping one eye on the lookout for celebrities.

If the emphasis in Carnaby Street shops was on fashion for the 'rockers', there were plenty of new shops for the 'mods' appearing on the King's Road, Chelsea. It was always worth a visit, not just to look at the latest styles but also to see the people parading along the pavement, who were pleased to be playing a part by spotting the leading fashion but upset when one of the shops was turned into a McDonald's. I photographed the window displays and copied styles from shoe shops including Ravel and Russell & Bromley, secretly dreaming that one day I would be able to justify putting a Timpson on the street. I realised my ambition in 2005 when we opened a shoe repair shop – next to McDonald's.

The 60s changed our social pecking order and put more power and influence into the hands of teenagers and trendy people in their twenties. Young fashion shops were opened and every high street had new shops just selling jeans, and outlets full of adventurous fashion that called themselves boutiques.

I tried to jump on the bandwagon by opening a clothes shop in the basement of our shoe shop in Market Street, Manchester and called it Shoetique. In 1970 hardly any shops put ladies shoes and clothes together (this was fifteen years before Next showed everyone how to sell coordinated fashion) so I was on to a good idea, but I was hopeless at buying clothes so the shop was a flop. Things didn't get much better even after we hired someone with fashion experience and opened three separate Shoetique shops around Manchester – they never made any money.

*

Most fashion retailers tried to cater for the new wave of young fashion but few realised that this meant a fundamental change to the look and layout of their shops. One chain that captured the mood was Lewis Separates.

Lewis Separates was one of many other women's fashion

chains that were developed after the Second World War. By 1965, Bernard Lewis and his three brothers had built a business of 70 shops. Faced with the fashion revolution the Lewises made a bold move by changing the whole chain to a new format under the Chelsea Girl fascia, a name chosen to reflect the influence of the King's Road. It was an inspired move that instantly created the UK's first chain of fashion boutiques.

In the late 1980s Bernard Lewis did it again. By then the mood had moved away from boutiques, with Next and the Burton Group opening shops based on more sophisticated design. Chelsea Girl was looking dated, the swinging 60s had long since disappeared and Bernard Lewis decided Chelsea Girl had to go. The stores were converted to River Island, a brilliant transformation which has kept the business in the forefront of fashion shopping ever since and remains totally owned by the family's Lewis Trust Group.

Each generation brings exciting new fashion formats like Jack Wills, AllSaints and Hollister which have yet to show they can adapt from one generation to another. It isn't easy for a fashion store to consistently keep in tune with its customers.

Shop design, helpful staff, prime locations, an efficient distribution system and well organised administration all help, but if the buyers miss the boat, one poor season can put a fashion chain in long-term difficulty.

Perhaps the longest running young fashion survivor is Top Shop, which started life as a department within a Peter Robinson store but really blossomed in the 1970s and 80s as a leading part of Ralph Halpern's Burton project. The brand was regularly updated under the guidance of shop designer Rodney Fitch. More recently Philip Green has taken a shine to Top Shop, putting a lot of his own time into it and developing a design link with Kate Moss which has helped to launch the brand in New York.

Another long-term fashion survivor is Monsoon with their companion brand Accessorize. City analysts and fund managers may have found it a frustrating business – it was floated and then privatised and there have been a couple of periods when profits collapsed, but to me it is a great business with a good property portfolio and well managed shops doing a distinctive job on the high street. I am a real fan because Accessorize has proved to be the perfect place to purchase successful stocking fillers for my wife, Alex, at Christmas.

Peter Simon, a trader on Portobello Road market who originated from Sri Lanka, opened his first Monsoon shop in 1973 in Beauchamp Place. With his emphasis on oriental styling and strong colours Monsoon had hippy fashion appeal. When Accessorize followed in 1984, next door to Monsoon in Covent Garden, the same disciplined approach to buying and displays was used to produce a tight range of coordinated accessories that was laid out in a way that made shopping easy.

Despite the occasional profit warning and battles in the boardroom, Monsoon hasn't lost any of the freshness it brought to shopping centres 40 years ago.

Stephen Marks kept his company French Connection in the public eye and on the young fashion shopping list by the controversial but effective use of its fcuk logo. Despite its many critics, the logo made a massive difference. Most of my top retailers put their personality into the business and are happy to be at the forefront of the company publicity. It was a courageous risk for Stephen Marks to personally back the decision to use fcuk as the face of his business. It magnified the company profile several times over, but even the strongest marketing still relies on the store stocking the right styles year after year.

Bernard Lewis, Peter Simon and Stephen Marks have all been able to stay in touch with young fashion for over twenty years. Few others have that ability, so it is highly likely that the biggest selling fashion fascias of 2040 have not yet even been invented.

RALPH HALPERN

In the late 1970s, before Ralph Halpern masterminded a major miracle, most market analysts had written off Burton the Tailor as a basket case. It was yesterday's business, starting to lose money and likely to get a lot worse. The only feature that propped up the share price was the property portfolio.

Fortunately Burton had bought Peter Robinson, a ladies' wear fashion chain that included a fabulous freehold on Oxford Circus along with about 30 stores across the country. The properties were well worth buying, but hidden on the Peter Robinson payroll was another major asset, Ralph Halpern, who joined as a trainee in 1961.

Peter Robinson developed a young fashion department in their Sheffield store under the name Top Shop. It captured the 60s mood and was spread to other stores. When Ralph Halpern became Burton's chief executive in 1976 he already had plans for a retail revolution and Top Shop gave him a clear idea of the way to go.

Ralph Halpern's larger-than-life character attracted and developed a new breed of fashion retailers, men and women who were on a mission. Burton was a big chain of shops with a fast declining band of loyal customers. Made-to-measure two- and three-piece suits were OK for dad and grandpa but young people in the 60s and 70s wanted to break with tradition. Top Shop was the right sort of store for the new generation.

But Halpern's Burton revolution wasn't just about young fashion. He created a range of clothing shops that covered most parts of the mass market. Top Man catered for the Top Shop customer's boyfriend. He bought Dorothy Perkins to give sharp fashions a wider age appeal, and Evans (formerly Evans Outsize) which smartened up styles for the fuller figure. Later, wanting to capture customers from Next and Richard Shops, Halpern's team created 'Principles' (which at the prototype stage had a clever graphic as a logo instead of a name).

Halpern's design guru was Rodney Fitch who drew up a lifestyle blueprint for every brand. Fitch was a class act (he also designed the Asda logo that is still used 35 years later). Halpern had help from a team of potential superstars; the Burton executives were constantly pursued by headhunters and many went on to run some of Britain's top retailers. They had a new language to describe this new breed of shops. 'A focused offer that attacks a clearly defined target market with a design-led solution'. Some might sneer at the gobbledegook but Halpern produced shops that were miles more exciting than Burton and attracted loads of extra customers. He even managed to put some new sparkle into the core Burton shops, where shirts, ties, jeans and knitwear and ready-to-wear suits almost entirely replaced the old bespoke tailoring.

Halpern lived the dream and put his own personality at the centre of their publicity. His macho laddish approach, demonstrated by joining sex symbol Fiona Richmond at the opening of new Top Man stores, didn't go down too well with straight-laced institutional shareholders but it certainly produced plenty of publicity. Some thought he was pretty pleased with himself but he certainly had plenty to be pleased about. (It still rankles slightly, though, that he kept me waiting for nearly an hour for a lunch date to discuss the concessions Timpson were putting into Dorothy Perkins and Top Shop.)

Ralph Halpern rescued Burton from almost certain closure and created a group that looked likely to dominate the high street for decades. He made the most of the Burton property portfolio, refitting many of the original shops and converting others into Top Shop, Top Man, or a combination of the two. These conversions included the original Peter Robinson on Oxford Circus.

Halpern started adding to his property portfolio like a monopoly player buying every opportunity on the board. When Woolworths disposed of some shops in the mid-1980s Halpern snapped up several sites and converted them into a row of Burton Group fascias. Suddenly, Grove Street, Wilmslow, went from no Burton shops at all to having a full set.

The next move was to buy Debenhams, a substantial but sleepy department store chain that Halpern saw as the ideal candidate for a design-led revolution and the perfect place to put concessions selling all the Burton Group brands. The acquisition in 1985 was, he said, part of his multi-brand strategy and Harvey Nichols was the next name on his list. The timing wasn't great – after several good years consumer spending was heading for a downturn. Redesigning a big store is an expensive exercise and Halpern found that department store trading is different from multiple retailing.

With one of every fascia on nearly every main shopping street, Halpern started to pay more attention to property development, building new shopping precincts like The Orchard Centre, Dartford. It was unfortunate timing. With retailers starting to suffer it was difficult to let sites and some of the new developments had a full set of Burton fascias but still had plenty of empty shops. With property having to be written down in the balance sheet, Halpern came in for considerable City criticism and in 1992 the Board decided that he had to pay for developing expensive shopping centres after the market had peaked. Halpern was replaced by John Hoerner, who Halpern had brought in to run Debenhams. The shareholders seemed to ignore the amazing transformation Halpern had created (under his watch the market capitalisation grew from £50m to £1.8bn). Not for the first time, institutional shareholders acted like football fans and at the first sign of a loss of form called for a change of management. Ten years later the business was worth only £80m. Analysts sitting in their City offices are not always in the best position to dictate how retail experts should run a business.

Ralph Halpern had the flair to change the face of a big chunk of the high street. He attracted the following of a new shopping generation, but at the first hint of failure institutional shareholders preferred to back a 'safe pair of hands'. Burton would probably have done a lot better if they had continued to trust the man who had made Burton such a big business.

GEORGE DAVIES

The launch of the first Next branches in February 1982 was one of the most exciting events during my 50-plus years in retailing. I was just a casual observer, but for all those closely involved the creation of this brand-new retail concept must have been fantastic. Success was instant. Imagine the thrill when the Next team saw the first week's sales figures and realised they had a monster in the making. The opening of Next changed the direction of UK fashion retailing and, after over 30 years, Next remains a market leader.

Rightly, much of the credit for creating Next goes to George Davies, but he was not alone. He was, however, the vital link in a small team that put the concept together.

The thinking started at County Bank, the merchant banking arm of NatWest and advisers to Hepworth, who like other multiple tailors were wondering how to cope with a declining market. Hepworth chairman, Terence Conran, keen to develop something entirely new, involved Trevor Morgan, who, with a sound knowledge of the retail property market, joined the Hepworth Board following their acquisition of the 150-store Turners Shoes of which Trevor had been chief executive. They found the perfect vehicle, Kendall Rainwear, a tired 110-shop chain owned by Combined English Stores, who were keen to sell. Hepworth wanted to create a coordinated ladies' fashion chain, but with a management team experienced in menswear they needed to find a chief executive for the project. County Bank recommended George Davies who learnt his fashion retail skills at Littlewoods and was currently the driving force behind a Tupperware-style home-based fashion retailer called Pippa Dee. George Davies joined Hepworth, the Kendall Rainwear deal was done with Combined English Stores and a bewildered world of retailers wondered what would happen next.

Conran, Davies and Trevor Morgan didn't need any market research: their vision was based on design rather than statistics. The styles all related to each other, encouraging customers to mix and match so that instead of picking one garment they were persuaded to buy a complete outfit. With Terence Conran heading the team there was no need for a shop designer; the look had a bit of Habitat with wooden fixtures which were first put together as a prototype in Trevor Morgan's garage. Trevor was paranoid about paying as little as possible and with the shops averaging less than 1,000 square feet the first Next shops were fitted out at around £25,000 each – pretty amazing value, even in 1982.

Every fortnight a few more Kendall Rainwear shops were converted to Next and customers loved them. I watched the queue of customers waiting to pay in Grove Street, Wilmslow, in a shop that a few weeks earlier was taking less than 10 per cent of the Next turnover. We all looked in awe as each Next pulled in crowds of customers, but had no idea that George Davies had much bigger plans in mind. When all the Kendall shops had been converted, Davies had to find a way to expand his golden idea.

Next for Men was a natural development but the big move that totally dealt with Hepworth's problems was to convert the core tailoring shops to a big shop version of Next. It was a bold move; Hepworth sites were several times larger than the Kendall

Rainwear shops so these new versions of Next lacked the original intimacy of the Next design. But they worked, and when I saw Hepworth were closing on Regent Street in London to be converted to Next, I knew that George Davies had become the prime mover at Hepworth plc, who made him chief executive.

There was no stopping George's appetite for new ideas. In quick succession he launched Next Interiors, Next Accessories, a Next range of jewellery, Next Childrenswear and, perhaps his most forward thinking idea, the Next Directory, which eventually bridged the gap between mail order catalogues and internet shopping. George was a clever retailer, a showman who loved drama as demonstrated by his blockbuster post-Christmas sales that started at 6.00am on 28 December after three days of sale posters blocking the shop windows. His bold technique produced long queues across the country and spectacular sales that cleared the shelves for the next season.

To satisfy his appetite for growth, in 1987 George Davies obtained Salisbury Handbags and Zales by acquiring Combined English Stores, the company that had sold Kendall Rainwear to Hepworth. With the help of Roger Seelig at Morgan Grenfell, he engineered what amounted to a merger with Grattan Mail Order to provide the Next Directory with the infrastructure to quickly become a big player in the home shopping market. To complete the Next Collection, Davies opened a few shops called Next to Nothing to clear slow-moving merchandise from across the group and in a bizarre move, also in 1987, he bought Dillons the Newsagent to help distribute the Next Directory.

While George Davies was dreaming up more and more wacky ideas he was blessed with a very sophisticated stock control system and an exceptionally talented fashion buyer, Liz Devereux-Bachelor, who later became the second Mrs George

Davies. Through Trevor Morgan, who was the Chairman of the Timpson Management Buyout, I met the geeks behind Next's state-of-the-art stock control. Their chief guru showed considerable foresight when he told me, 'We have the most sophisticated merchandising system, but every growing business can expect to "hit the wall". The way management copes with their first major disaster will determine whether they can create a long-term future.'

George Davies was so busy dreaming up the next big Next idea he failed to forecast the fall in trading profit. The late 1980s were getting tough for all retailers and the adventurous George Davies was taking too many risks. He hit the wall in style and the Next share price slumped to 7p. After the merger with Next, Grattan Finance Director David Jones became chairman with George Davies as his chief executive. It was David Jones who reacted to City pressure and fired George Davies, putting himself in executive control. George Davies left Next on 8 December 1988.

The sack from his brainchild, Next, didn't stop George Davies from finding more new retail ideas. He was given the perfect opportunity by Archie Norman, chief executive of Asda, who invited George to create a new range of clothing for their supermarkets. Some wondered how George would cope with this shift downmarket but his range, branded 'George at Asda', was an instant success. His involvement gave the Asda team a focus and level of confidence that helped 'George at Asda' become the key to establishing a significant non-food business throughout the chain. The direct association came to an end in 2000 when Asda was acquired by Walmart but the 'George' brand continued growing to become one of the biggest labels in the UK and is spreading to Walmart worldwide.

A similar arrangement with Marks & Spencer became George Davies' most lucrative venture. Top M&S executives, Luc Vandevelde and Roger Holmes, were faced with a disastrous drop in ladies' fashion sales, a falling share price and disgruntled shareholders. They asked George Davies to help. His answer was to design, source and supply a more fashionable range than the staple M&S styling under the brand 'Per Una'. It worked. The combination of Davies and M&S created a lot of attention in the media and 'Per Una', launched in 2001, was an instant hit, attracting new customers to M&S and quickly taking 10 per cent of their women's wear business.

When Stuart Rose was fending off the takeover bid for M&S by Philip Green three years later, the royalty deal with Davies was attacked by Green and was seen by merchant banks as an inconvenient obstacle which stood in the way of the M&S defence. As a result a deal was done with Davies, who sold all his rights to 'Per Una' for £125m, easily his biggest payday.

No one expected Davies to stop inventing new retail concepts, but his next major venture, GIVe, a mixture of high street and online, with a proportion of profits going to charity, wasn't a success. The 25 shops opened in 2009 were closed two years later.

By creating Next, George Davies did the British consumer a big favour, and his flair put extra life into Asda and M&S. Despite the disappointment and the personal cost of GIVe, it seems unlikely that George Davies has devised his last new concept. But the Asda experience, compared with Next, suggests that he is at his best when he concentrates on dreaming up the ideas and creating fashion while someone else is left to do the day-to-day shopkeeping.

THE NEXT MIRACLE

David Jones and Simon Wolfson

When the Next plc share price fell below 10p in 1988 few would have expected an accountant to have the ability to rescue a fast fashion business, but David Jones did the job beyond everyone's expectations. He was the Finance Director of Kays at the age of 23 but quickly escaped from accountancy when Great Universal Stores made him chief executive of their key subsidiary BMO (British Mail Order). He was headhunted in 1982 to become chief executive of Grattan, which was taken over by Next in 1986. He became chairman of the enlarged group and after George Davies was ousted at the end of 1988 David took on the chief executive role of a company most people thought was heading into administration. He confounded the critical expert analysts by moving the Next market value from £25m in 1988 to £3.5bn when he retired in 2006.

Most, in his position, would have looked for a short-term solution to create the maximum immediate value for shareholders, who would have been delighted with a quick sale that produced anything in excess of £200m, but David Jones was looking a lot further ahead.

The eccentric loss makers created during George Davies' orgy of new ideas were clear candidates for closure. Without damaging the balance sheet Jones said goodbye to all the wacky and fringe developments, including Next Jewellery and the Next Gardening Directory. While realising the urgent need to clear out the major mistakes Jones also recognised the strength of the core Next concept and the massive potential of the Next Directory.

His toughest decision was to sell Grattan, a business in which he had invested a lot of his life and personal passion. Fortunately he found a ready buyer in the Germany-based company Otto Versand, who were keen to put Grattan together with Freemans mail order to form Otto UK. They paid £165m in 1999 for a business Next had acquired two years earlier for £300m. Despite this drop in price it was a good deal that strengthened Next finances and signalled the start of a simple strategy that has been followed for the last 25 years. Jones described his plan as 'One brand with two ways of shopping' but with the Next Directory being perfectly placed to trade over the internet, a third way of shopping is now a very important part of the brand.

David Jones not only picked the perfect strategy, he also developed a team with the talent to put his plan into practice. Next stores were never allowed to be second rate, Jones was never tempted to cut corners to save money and increase short-term profit; the core business always set high standards of shopfitting, presentation and housekeeping. The brand has always been aspirational but affordable – distinctive styles combining quality and value. When the original shops were opened by George Davies and the Hepworth team in 1982 they were clearly designed by 'one pair of eyes'. The same consistency continued throughout Next's financial roller coaster – the present eminence of the Next brand owes a lot to the stubborn way Jones stuck to these basic principles.

While overseeing all these dramatic changes David Jones was quietly coping with the early stages of his Parkinson's Disease which had been diagnosed in 1982. He handed over the chief executive role in 2001 but continued as chairman until 2006. The less successful involvement he then had with JJB Sports should not obscure the fact that David Jones rescued, revived and developed the most successful fashion chain in the UK.

*

It wasn't surprising that a few eyebrows were raised in the City when Simon Wolfson was appointed to succeed David Jones as Next chief executive in 2001. Not only had his father been the Next chairman from 1990 to 1998 but Simon's boyish features made him look little more than twenty years old. In fact he was 33 and had already spent ten years with Next, starting as a shop assistant at the Kensington branch in 1991 and joining the Board of Directors in 1997. Despite this experience Simon was the youngest chief executive of a FTSE 100 company and was viewed with considerable suspicion. There was no need to be bothered; the market capitalisation has risen to nearly £11bn in 2015.

During Simon Wolfson's time as chief executive trading has been tough for many of his closest competitors. Analysts regularly talked about the 'squeezed middle'. During the recession new value retailers like Primark and top of the range brands such as Burberry did well, but as buyers divided into cut price or quality those placed in the middle ground, particularly M&S, started to suffer. In theory Next, sitting right in the middle of the market, was bound to be under pressure. But under Simon Wolfson's firm and consistent guidance Next just continued to get better and increase market share.

Quietly confident, Wolfson has been a master at reading economic trends and clearly communicating his thoughts. His trading statements have always been realistic and shown consistent political judgement. It was hardly surprising that, as an active Conservative Party supporter, he was invited to become a peer and is now Lord Wolfson of Aspley Guise.

In 1982 Next was born with a dramatic launch and during its first few years George Davies took a sequence of big risks in his desire to be the high street's leading innovator. David Jones and Simon Wolfson have taken the very best of the Next inventions and replaced the drama with consistently high standards in every aspect of the Next offer. This approach has helped Next overtake M&S on most meaningful measurements.

Wolfson's assured approach may not be as dramatic as life under George Davies but no one could describe Next as boring, particularly when they put on an end of season sale. Learning from the successful sales mounted in the 1980s the Next winter sale still starts at 6.00am on Boxing Day with customers starting to queue on Christmas Day.

It is amazing to think that in 1989 Next nearly went bust. David Jones and Simon Wolfson saved and nurtured a brand that has become one of Britain's best, and one which would be better placed than anyone else to acquire and rekindle Marks & Spencer.

PHILIP GREEN

Philip Green is nine years younger than me which explains why when I was a shoe buyer visiting the import agent Martin Geminder in about 1966 Philip's job was to make me a cup of coffee. The next time we met, nearly 40 years later, was the night Timpson eventually won a modest prize as Employer of the Year at The Retail Week Awards. Philip was the retail personality of the year, a justified accolade for someone who has been involved in so many retail names.

Philip Green has been good at buying and selling – not just the sourcing and marketing of fashion at which he brashly claims to be an instinctive expert, but the buying and selling of businesses. He now owns several highly profitable chains of shops but, unlike many of my retail legends, he didn't start any of the chains from scratch. His success has been created by a series of deals.

Green's blunt market trader style was established at an early age. The death of his father, when Philip was only twelve, and the example of his mother whose commercial flair developed one of the UK's earliest self-service petrol stations, may well have made him determined to build his own business. After a few false starts he had his first, crucial, big win. The high street was full of denim in a number of new chains selling jeans, with varying degrees of success. It was the perfect opportunity for Philip Green. In 1985 he bought a failing denim retailer, Jean Jeanie, for about £60,000 and within months his instinct as a trader turned it round and he was able to sell his stake for about £3m. He invested his capital gain in a quoted retail company Amber Day that sold designer clothing, trading as Woodhouse and Review. Green made a bold move when Amber Day acquired the Glasgow based cut price fashion chain What Everyone Wants in 1990 for £47m. It was a very distinctive business that attracted a lot of loyal customers by stocking up-to-date popular fashion at rock bottom prices. Green, as ever, took a personal interest in the detail and insisted on higher margins which reduced the turnover and led to a profit warning for Amber Day. This was the final straw for City shareholders who were already critical of Green's lack of respect for the corporate governance required in a public company. Green had to go.

Although he lost his job at Amber Day he made enough money from his severance pay and shareholding to move on to the next deal, having learnt that his talents are better suited to being part of a private business.

The Jean Jeanie experience showed him how to make money. Although his maverick style didn't appeal to institutional shareholders, bankers looking for private equity type deals found Green the perfect partner. With proven expertise at managing troubled retail chains they were keen to back Green if he could pay a pittance for a poorly performing business with plenty of potential to respond to his retailing skill. He went on to do a series of leveraged deals that could be labelled 'management buy-ins'.

His first deal after Amber Day was the purchase from the receiver in 1993 of a chain called Parker and Franks, a trading name he quickly changed to Xception, an odd value/fashion store that suited Green's market approach to retailing.

The leverage deals got progressively bigger and more ambitious. The purchase the following year of Owen Owen, the department store chain that also owned Lewis's Department Stores (not to be confused with John Lewis) was more about property than retailing. Some stores were sold to Allders and Debenhams before Philip Green sold his stake and moved on to the next deal.

He helped Tom Hunter buy Olympus Sport from British Shoe Corporation in 1995 which gave him a 13 per cent stake in Tom Hunter's Sports Division, which itself brought a big profit when the business was sold to JJB Sports three years later for £290m.

The picture portrayed in the press suggests that Philip Green has been a one man show with a tough, uncompromising attitude to his employees, but even Philip Green would never have been able to create so much success on his own. Tom Hunter was one of his fellow travellers and Green's wife Tina, who has been the family shareholder, seems to have provided a regular return to reality.

Green might have learnt some tough lessons at What Everyone Wants (WEW) but he also discovered some loyal talent. Ian Grabiner, who ran WEW and later also worked for Tom Hunter, became Green's right-hand man many years later. Elaine Gray (later Elaine McPherson) was a young buyer at WEW who followed Green to his next acquisition in 1996: Mark One, a dull looking range of fashion shops that was making a loss and which Green rescued from the receiver. After the business had been put back in profit, Green's exit came in 2004 via a management buyout to the senior team, including

Elaine McPherson, who were able to sell the business to the Iceland-based Baugur for £55m.

After Mark One the deals got a lot bigger, starting with the rump of Sears in 1999, the conglomerate created by Charles Clore. Philip Green claims to have spotted the potential nine years earlier. I too was part of a consortium that ran a slide rule over the Sears portfolio but Green did the deal we didn't.

When Sears broke up the remaining shops in British Shoe Corporation after their disastrous deal with Stephen Hinchcliffe's fantasy Facia group had left them with a lot of unwanted sites, Philip Green picked up a sizeable portfolio of Curtess, Freeman Hardy Willis, and Trueform shops which he treated as a property deal. He aggressively attacked the portfolio to turn it into cash as I discovered to my cost as a tenant in a number of sites including one in Ilford. We were given legal notice to quit and when I pleaded for enough time to find another site the agent's instructions were to tell John Timpson to f... off! Philip has a clear and colourful way of making his point.

When the last bit of Sears was up for sale, Green was well prepared. He had financial backing from the Barclay brothers who quickly got more than their money back when the fashion shops (Richard Shops, Warehouse, Wallis and Miss Selfridge were sold to Arcadia – formerly the Burton Group). It is estimated that the Sears deal produced a profit of £150m within nine months.

The next deal was bigger still and was the start of a significant relationship with Bank of Scotland. Green bought British Home Stores (BHS) from Storehouse for £200m, putting in £20m of his own money while bank finance sorted the rest. Although the stores didn't look much different, within months

Green claimed new merchandise was pushing up sales, but it was mainly cost-cutting, better margins and longer credit from suppliers that helped to improve cash flow. The acquisition went so well Tina Green got £400m in dividends over the next four years

A happy Bank of Scotland was ready to back the next Green deal, which was the purchase of Arcadia, the residue of the Burton Group after the sale of Debenhams but including the shops Green had sold to them a few years before. This was a dream deal. Green's personal equity investment was only £9.2m but three years later the dividend was £1.2bn. The bank was so supportive they were happy to fund the dividend in return for an additional loan agreement.

Arcadia was perfect for Philip Green, the fashion chain of his dreams which let him put all his flair and flamboyance into practice, with the added bonus of show business connections including Kate Moss.

If you list all the fascias I have already connected with Philip Green it would be possible to fill a shopping centre, but he still had plans to get bigger and the target was Marks & Spencer – and he very nearly got it.

Since failing in his bid to buy M&S the feverish deal activity has died down. Philip Green started to look overseas where he has had some success and the Arcadia chains continued to perform well at home. BHS, however, never looked loved and, after several years of trading losses, the business was sold to a specially created company called Retail Acquisitions, run by Dominic Chappell, a man with roots in Monaco who seems to know more about racing driving than retailing. In his press release, Green referred to the sale as an 'honest deal' – I suspect it will lead to the end of BHS as we know it.

In assessing his track record as a retailer it is wrong to be blinkered by the show biz side of Philip Green. The extravagant parties with celebrity guests and his Monaco lifestyle are an inevitable part of his character. His maverick style, criticised in the early days by Private Eye and City institutions, has been a hallmark of his success. By learning from the Amber Day experience and sticking to private businesses he has been able to use his talent as a wheeler dealer to make phenomenal capital gains for himself and his bankers. It is difficult to think of anyone else who has been involved with and turned round so many retail chains. At times he will have been a tough employer and he drove a hard bargain with plenty of his suppliers, but while many other retailers have closed their doors Philip Green continues to flourish.

SIR CHARLES CLORE

Inever met the man who probably had as big an influence as anyone on my career.

Charles Clore was the son of an East End of London tailor who fled from Russia to escape a wave of anti-Semitism. Despite his background he didn't make his money out of tailoring but, almost by chance, became the UK's biggest shoe retailer with nearly 30 per cent of the market.

Clore's prime interest was property and he spotted that many of the multiple retailers that grew between the two world wars had substantial, but undervalued, freehold portfolios sitting on the balance sheet. A perfect example was Sears Ltd which traded as Trueform and Freeman Hardy Willis. In the early 1950s, lacklustre trading produced only modest profits and Clore was able to buy Sears for considerably less than the property value. Clore bought the London shoe chain Clerkenwell Footwear (which then changed its name to Curtess) from experienced shoe retailer Harry Levison, who then joined Sears. With Levison aboard and lending his experience, Clore was able to develop Sears by selling a few freeholds and funding a shop development programme.

Clore repeated the property-based acquisition formula when he bought Dolcis and Manfield in 1956 and Saxone, Lilley & Skinner in 1962 which included a spectacular freehold – Lilley & Skinner on Oxford Street, London, the biggest shoe shop in the world. The shoe businesses were brought together and called British Shoe Corporation with an enormous warehouse and office complex at Braunstone near Leicester.

Further expansion in the footwear market was thwarted in 1964 by the Ziff family whose Stylo business beat Clore in a bidding battle for Barratts Footwear, and a final block on further shoe business acquisition came when a bid to buy Timpson, my family business, was referred to the Monopolies and Mergers Commission. The rival bid from UDS Group wasn't referred and Clore never tried to buy another shoe chain.

As property was the main driver behind his deals Clore was happy to buy any sort of shop. His next deal, the purchase of the Liverpool based chain of Lewis's Department Stores (not to be confused with John Lewis) included probably the most prime retail property in Britain, Selfridges on Oxford Street, London.

Further acquisitions included William Hill the bookmakers and Mappin and Webb the jewellers.

Charles Clore changed the world of retail property. Today freeholds are mainly in the hands of institutional investors with retailers paying the market rent. Most of the retail portfolios, like the one built by my grandfather in the 1930s, have been sold and leased back or grabbed by an opportunistic asset stripper.

Charles Clore changed the world of footwear retailing and that is how he shaped my career. Before he built up British Shoe Corporation Timpson was the market leader throughout the North of England and Scotland. I have little doubt that without that competition Timpson would have flourished for much longer and I would never have had the foresight to sell our shoe shops and concentrate on our current service business.

It didn't feel like it at the time, but while Charles Clore was dominating the high street he was also doing me a big favour.

THE RISE AND FALL OF BRITISH SHOE

Harry Levison created British Shoe Corporation, one of the few businesses ever to totally dominate a retail market. But, within fifteen years of him handing over control, the business went into free fall.

Harry Levison joined Charles Clore shortly after the purchase of Sears Ltd in 1955 and for the next twenty years Levison created a business that captured nearly 30 per cent of the UK retail shoe trade. His vision and flair must make him a candidate for the brightest talent ever seen on the high street.

We, at Timpson and all the other footwear multiples suffered from his expertise. We found it tough to trade against such a dominant and competent competitor. None of our shops was more than a few doors away from one of Harry Levison's fascias.

The way he built such a colossal category killer could be the perfect case study for today's marketing students. Although he used computers and automation when the enormous distribution centre was opened in Braunstone near Leicester, in the formative years Harry Levison had little help from technology and I doubt whether he did much market research. He was a true entrepreneur making decisions based on flair and experience.

He had the help of a good management team, in the field

and at his head office but the key creators of the British Shoe success were the buyers. Levison had grown his own business, Clerkenwell Footwear, which he sold to Sears and converted into Curtess. Shoe buying was in his blood; he learnt the tricks of the trade by being a buyer and working in shops selling the shoes he had bought. He wasn't trained at a fashion college, he learnt on the job, so it wasn't surprising that he picked buyers by spotting people already in the business who had the flair to find the best sellers. Once he had appointed a good buyer he didn't interfere, but he always knew what was selling.

Charles Clore's acquisitions gave Levison a comprehensive range of brands that covered all but the very top end of the shoe market. Customers looking for quality had Saxone and Lilley & Skinner, young fashion customers shopped at Dolcis, the mass market was catered for by both Trueform and Freeman Hardy Willis, and Curtess was the cut price chain. Manfield, sitting right in the middle, was the only one that didn't have a clear market identity. British Shoe Corporation had a set of shops for every high street. Ellesmere Port and Skegness would have Trueform, Freeman Hardy Willis and Curtess, while on Oxford Street, London you would just see Dolcis, Saxone and Lilley & Skinner. Most city centres would have at least one of every fascia and in some places there were three British Shoe shops next door to each other.

It was a big advantage to know what was selling in so many markets, particularly for the cheaper chains that continually copied the best styles from Saxone and Dolcis. I only saw the Timpson statistics; a sight of sales elsewhere would have been invaluable.

Buying shoes can be a bit of a nightmare, even if you know what you are doing. Fashion has a habit of springing surprises and so does the climate. Boots and sandals rely on snow and sun: without seasonal weather you are left with too much stock and lots of mark downs. Every buyer hopes to find the most popular styles in the bestselling colours but nothing is certain until the first deliveries hit the shops. Buyers are always wrong; they have too much stock of the slow sellers and never have enough of the winners (to make things worse repeat orders can arrive too late, when fashion has moved on to the next phase).

It doesn't help having to cater for so many different sized feet. We provided women's shoes from size 3 to 8 and men's 6 to 12, both with half sizes, but still regularly heard the complaint 'You never have my size'. Children's shoes were even trickier if you catered for width fittings, but the British Shoe 'Birthday' brand left the proper fitting business to Clarks.

British Shoe promoted two other brands, 'Vanguard' basic value shoes in Trueform and Freeman Hardy Willis, and Hush Puppies which were sold on an exclusive UK licence and were also sold in Saxone. The only brand common to most value multiples was 'Tuf', the first moulded rubber sole styles to carry a six-month guarantee. We discovered the downside in Hamilton near Glasgow where our Timpson shop was next door to Trueform. The day before our auditors arrived for stock taking the Trueform manager 'lent' his Tuf stock to our manager, who returned the favour just before the stock was due to be counted in Trueform.

With such a big share of the market British Shoe could make or break their suppliers. Some factories sold well over half their production to British Shoe, including several shoe makers in Italy, Brazil and in the Far East. Their buyers used their power to insist on exclusivity, and preferential terms.

Some expected and received a range of personal perks which went well beyond the pub lunches I was given by my suppliers. I believe some received payments into Swiss and Brazilian bank accounts.

These benefits in kind were matched by one other British Shoe weakness: they had an arrogant attitude to customer care. Shops had to keep customer complaints below 2 per cent, but with some shoes falling to bits at the rate of 5 per cent or more, shop staff had to deal with a lot of unhappy customers.

The poor level of customer care at least gave us one area where we could compete, which is why we, at Timpson, produced our Code of Service, but British Shoe were so big they could afford to take customers for granted. However, backhanders accepted by some of the buyers eventually did the business a lot more damage.

After over twenty years in charge Levison handed over to Harry Harrison, a highly competent operations man who learnt his retailing with Littlewoods but had been with British Shoe long enough to totally get the culture. Sadly Harrison didn't get the chance to show he was the right man for the job. He died, suddenly, less than two years after taking on the role. His successor David Roberts was a tough member of the buying team who took charge just in time to face a frenetic period for footwear retailers (so bad I sold out!). As Tesco have found, it is difficult for anyone with 30 per cent of a market to grab a bigger share. Roberts was replaced by Chris Marsland, a nuts and bolts man with an administrative background whose appointment was designed to bring the buying department to heel. British Shoe had moved a long way away from the methods of Harry Levison.

The business still found a few ways to grow with

concessions in other Sears stores like Wallis and Miss Selfridge, a new out-of-town concept branded 'Shoe City', and 'Olympus Sport', an ambitious bid to establish the best sports shop on the high street.

I got the first hint that all was not great in 1989 when Timpson bought British Shoe's shoe repair business, a rag bag of concessions inside a few Saxone and Curtess shops, a couple of Co-op stores, Lewis's Department Stores and a busy branch in the basement of Selfridges. The shoe repair business had been badly run, but in turning it round I had the chance to see lots of British Shoe shops on the inside. I discovered falling sales, low morale and a lack of investment. The brash confidence of the original British Shoe had disappeared.

It wasn't just British Shoe that was suffering. The rest of Sears Holdings was also in difficulty and the Board responded by appointing a new chief executive, Liam Strong, previously marketing and operations director of British Airways. As I was no longer involved in shoe shops I went to see him, somewhat arrogantly thinking that he would find my experience helpful. I came away wondering whether he knew anything about retailing, but he did ask me to go and see Ian Thompson, a South African who he had just appointed as the new British Shoe managing director.

I had tea with Ian Thompson while he told me how he was going to solve the problems facing British Shoe.

Ian didn't need any advice, he'd already worked it all out. 'We just need to go for the easy wins' he told me. 'I'm concentrating on Dolcis and Shoe Express – one is the fashion leader, the other a price leader, both are category killers.'

I tried to point out that Trueform, Freeman Hardy Willis and Saxone had a fantastic following from everyday customers but I think he had some marketing advice and a bit of research that proved he must be right.

Ian Thompson was certainly single-minded; he threw his efforts behind Dolcis and Shoe Express and abandoned the other brands.

The strategy was risky. Dolcis could only continue as the leading young fashion brand if the shops stocked the most fashionable shoes. To do that they needed the best buyers. But some of the best buyers in the business no longer worked for British Shoe.

Having been a shoe buyer myself I know that when business is bad the buyer is the first to get the blame. When process and administration replaced flair at the top of British Shoe it was inevitable that the buying team would come under the microscope. The introduction of stock controllers and merchandisers put a lot of power in the hands of clever but inexperienced new staff in their twenties and the buying job was downgraded. The change in structure and a clampdown on perks from key suppliers led to many buyers finding their happiness elsewhere. British Shoe said goodbye to the buyers who had helped build the business just when they were needed to justify the faith they had in Dolcis.

The faith that Ian Thompson, and presumably Liam Strong, had in Shoe Express was equally misplaced.

Shoe Express was copied from the Payless format that was spectacularly successful in the USA. When I met Ian Thompson the totally self-service concept had just been successfully tested in St Helens where a Trueform shop was converted to the new format and sales jumped by 40 per cent. The results were misleading. The new shop opened with every size available in every bestselling style, the best staff in the area, a brand new refit and the top brass from head office hovering to make sure nothing went wrong. Subsequent conversions to Shoe Express did decent business but none matched the success of St Helens. By the time the 100th Shoe Express was opened most of the British Shoe team realised that they hadn't got the winner they first expected.

It got worse. Neither Sears nor British Shoe seemed to recognise that so much of their past success was due to great buyers. Flair was replaced with process, and buyers became mere style pickers with more power given to the stock controllers and merchandisers. As sales fell, especially in the unloved Saxone, Manfield, Trueform and Freeman Hardy Willis, British Shoe management was locked in continual meetings and seldom went out to shops to find out what was really going on.

When, in 1995, Olympus Sport was sold for £1 (with debts of £30m) to Tom Hunter with the backing of Philip Green, we should have seen the signs that the fabulous British Shoe empire was about to collapse, but few would have forecast the deal they did to run away from the chains that were no longer loved.

They handed over the management of Saxone, Manfield, Trueform and Freeman Hardy Willis to Stephen Hinchcliffe, an inexperienced retailer who was gathering a motley collection of unprofitable retail chains including Sock Shop and Salisbury Handbags. In a bizarre deal British Shoe sort of lent the business to Hinchcliffe without bothering to find out too much about him. Two years later they got all the shops back (in a desperate state) and Hinchcliffe was on the way to prison for fraud.

With everything going so wrong the final act was carried out by company doctor, David James, who inevitably decided the only way to sort out Sears was to sell off all the parts. British Shoe never made it to the New Millennium.

No one has ever really explained how a business that had nearly 30 per cent of the market imploded within five years of Liam Strong and Ian Thompson launching their development plan. Perhaps the market no longer needed so many shoe shops. Maybe the business got too big for its own good. It could be argued that letting the buyers go was a fatal own goal. Or perhaps Harry Levison had created an organisation that only he could run.

Whatever went wrong at British Shoe, it would never have had the chance to produce such a dramatic downfall if Harry Levison hadn't created such a fantastic business in the first place.

THE SHOE SHOP SURVIVORS

A few years ago I played a bizarre game with my long-time friend, retired shoe manufacturer Thomas Black. We called the game 'Shoe Shops' and the rules were simple: whoever won the toss named a UK chain of ten or more shoe shops that has traded at some time during the last 50 years. The opponent named another, and the game continued until one of us couldn't think of another brand. On one occasion we listed an amazing 72 different businesses, all specialising in footwear (shops like M&S, Littlewoods and department stores that sold shoes were disallowed). Given the number of shoe chains it isn't surprising that on some streets there were three, four or even, in one case I saw, five shoe shops standing next door to each other. Nor was it a surprise, with extra competition coming from training shoes, mail order and shoe concessions in fashion stores, that most of the names in our game have gone out of business. Here are a few that are now extinct – Saxone, Dolcis, Curtess, Hiltons, Oliver, Frisby, Tylers, Bayne & Duckett, Lennards, Englands, Tandem, Wyles, Turners, Easiephit, Manfield, Trueform, Freeman Hardy Willis, J.W. Wassal and, of course, Timpson.

With such a long list of casualties, I've considerable admiration for those that have survived and still make money out of mainly selling shoes.

Many of the high-priced top fashion stores that littered

Bond Street – where, in the 1970s, I furtively photographed shop windows hoping to copy the latest styles at a fraction of the price – still survive. But Kurt Geiger, Magli, Charles Jourdan and Jimmy Choo are part of the international set and didn't have the ten UK shops needed to qualify for our game.

Today a few fashion shoe chains still flourish, but most are relative newcomers. Dune was founded in 1992 and now sells its elegant, classic styling in about 50 shops and 170 concessions. Schuh, a bold and lively young fashion concept that grew from a single shop opened in Edinburgh in 1981, now has 100 shops and can certainly claim to be the most consistently successful of the fashion shoe specialists. Sandy Alexander, who created the business, really went for it – the shoes and the decor were completely different from any other shoe shop and customers clearly shared the Schuh buyers' taste in fashion. The business blossomed at the time typical shoe chains like Timpson were treading water and I wandered round Schuh outlets full of jealousy and admiration. After a management buyout in 1990 the chain was sold to Genesco in 2011 for £125m. A great exit compared with many other shoe shops that went into administration.

Office also started trading in 1981 as a concession in Knightsbridge before opening a stand-alone shop on The King's Road three years later. Like Schuh, Office hit the right fashion theme: their buyers, led by art student Richard Wharton, had an excellent eye for fresh fast fashion that was bought in bulk and displayed with authority.

When you look at a shop that is on top of the game, the style selection looks so simple and obvious. Shoe buyers not only have to see style trends in advance, they need to back their judgement boldly and also need a bit of luck. It doesn't take much to miss a new trend, invest in the wrong styles and have a poor season. Buyers are often backed up by merchandisers who study past sales figures to predict future trends, but no system can forecast the next turn of the fashion cycle and a street-wise buyer will make better decisions than a powerful computer. In the fashion game everyone is bound to have the odd bad season, which, if misunderstood by analysts and investors, can lead to a loss of confidence and the removal of the talented people who had been the original source of success. Office had some tricky years but kept close to their original concept while nearest competitor, Faith, failed to negotiate the fickle fortunes of fashion and finished up in administration. Office now has over 100 shops and another 50 in-store concessions. After a period as part of Tom Hunter's empire the company was acquired by venture capitalists with Alan Leighton as non-executive chairman.

Another shoe company that prospered while most other footwear shops were floundering was L.K. Bennett, developed by Linda Bennett who had a particularly good feel for the elegant fashion that appealed to a new generation of Sloane Rangers. Starting with a small shop in Wimbledon then graduating to the King's Road, L.K. Bennett grew by opening smart department store concessions and bigger branches that extended the brand to clothing and could count the Duchess of Cambridge among her A-list celebrity customers. Linda Bennett built a business that was worth £70m in 2007 when she sold a 70 per cent stake to private equity.

*

These survivors are newcomers compared with Russell & Bromley, the most consistent shoe shop on the high street.

Russell & Bromley goes back to 1873 when George Bromley, who worked for a shoemaker in Lewes called Russell, married Elizabeth, his employer's daughter. The couple managed the family shop in Eastbourne, which became the first shop with Russell & Bromley above the door.

Russell & Bromley became a true family business in 1898 when George and Elizabeth's eldest son Frederick joined the company and bought a shop in Tonbridge. He found another in Sevenoaks, and started to steadily open shops and buy out shoe retailers from his base in Bromley. Frederick retired in 1936, handing over control to his sons Keith and Michael, who by the start of the Second World War had twenty branches.

The opening of a shop in Bond Street in 1947 declared the family's ambition to pursue the quality end of the market but the opportunist acquisitions of three generations had created a diverse range of properties, some of which were very different to Bond Street, London.

The critical move was made in 1968 when the family (Michael's children, Peter, Roger and Nicola were now involved) decided to close a quarter of the shops – those that were too small or down market. From then on Russell & Bromley have consistently set a high standard selling elegantly styled, quality shoes at a time when other shoe retailers introduced cheaper materials and increased margins. The shops were given spacious shopfits with nitpicking standards of housekeeping. Russell & Bromley always gave great personal service, especially in the children's departments and their separate children's shoe shops.

In the 1970s and 80s, through the Multiple Shoe Retailers' trade associations, I worked closely with Russell & Bromley's personnel and training controller John England-Crowther and got some insight into how carefully the business nurtured its reputation by delivering tip-top service.

They were the first business I encountered with a crystal-clear vision of what the business was about and where it was heading. They had a list of every town and city where they wanted a shop; not a long list but it included Chester, near my home. John asked me to keep an eye open for the right site, which I did for seven years, but the perfect spot didn't come on the market until fifteen years after they started looking. They were totally disciplined in sticking to their brief.

Russell & Bromley has survived and flourished by being a family business with high standards that constantly keeps the right range for their core customers and probably provides the best personal service in the UK.

*

When British Shoe Corporation imploded, the disappearance of Curtess, Shoe Express and Shoe City left a big gap at the bottom end of the shoe market. Brantana, a value shoe retailer from Belgium, and Deichmann with a 1,000-shop business in Germany both entered the UK market with their 'pairs on display' self-service technique which had been the main idea behind the Payless concept in the United States that British Shoe Corporation imported in the mid-1980s as the inspiration behind Shoe Express.

But selling bulk pairs of shoes by self-service had been happening in Blackburn, Lancashire many years before Payless ever put a pair on display.

Tommy Ball, who started in business as a rag and bone man, set up a discount shoe warehouse in Blackburn that attracted customers from all over North-West England.

Tommy was a maverick who didn't like rules, especially regulations that got in between him and his customers. While trading hours were still strictly regulated Tommy welcomed late-night shoppers and found innovative ways to get round Sunday Shopping laws.

All his shoes were strung up with string – a hole in the back of the heel was a sure sign the shoes had been bought from Tommy Ball.

*

If a shoe trade expert had been asked in 1985 who will be the big survivors, most would have guessed Clarks, but hardly anyone would have thought of Benson Shoe.

Benson Shoe was just another on my long list of shoe multiples, so well down the pecking order it would have been a good name to remember in my shoe shops game. In 1980, Benson Shoe had no more than 50 shops around Leicester and the Midlands selling ordinary shoes to everyday customers at fairly low prices.

Through a long-term investment the Smith family had a minority stake in Benson Shoe and, for reasons only they can understand, in 1980 brothers Michael and Christopher Smith bought the company. Fifty shops was clearly not enough to support a significant head office and warehouse and make a decent profit so the Smith family started to buy more shops, at a time when the whole of the multiple shoe trade was about to fall into turmoil. They acquired a similar cheap and cheerful Midlands chain, J.W. Wassall, in 1981 and in 1986 a slightly more upmarket chain, Tyler, with shops mainly in Ireland. The rest of the shoe world hardly noticed, but while British Shoe was collapsing due to their inexperienced management desperately doing their insecure deal with Stephen Hinchcliffe, the Smiths concentrated on the value market and rebranded the shops Discount Shoe Zone (later to become Shoe Zone). With the help of management recruited from Shoe City, the next Smith generation, Anthony and Charles, learnt how to sell pairs on display through self-service. In 2000, the business suddenly became significant. The acquisition of Oliver Shoes (the business that bought Timpson and also Hilton Shoes) added 258 shops to Benson for £6.1m and more than doubled the size of their business.

At a time when shoe companies were installing progressively more complicated computer systems and making less money, the Smiths ignored the latest ideas of best practice and did things their way. The buyers didn't have any young merchandisers working out budgets and buying targets, they could buy whatever they wanted as long as the company had no more than 500 styles in stock and stock levels were within a whisker of last year.

This simple formula worked. I have never thought their shoes looked particularly pretty, but what can you expect when most lines are less than £10 with a 60 per cent margin.

It worked so well that in 2007 Benson bought Shoefayre from the Co-op (another 250 shops) and the following year picked up Stead & Simpson.

In 1980 no one would have guessed that Benson Shoe would be able to float the business for the £80m that was achieved in May 2014. The Smith family come across as quiet retiring gentlefolk but they certainly set an example to the rest of us who struggled to make money by selling shoes.

*

Clarks were always an odds-on favourite to survive. Once they had acquired K Shoes in 1972 there was no other serious competitor selling middle-of-the-road shoes in the middle of the market.

Most UK kids are introduced to Clarks at an early age. My first shoes were fitted when shops used an X-ray machine, the Pedoscope, to measure my feet and show a detailed picture of every bone in the foot. These machines were just about to be banned for health and safety reasons when I started work as a shoe shop assistant in 1960. Four years later I was working at Clarks.

I was part of a graduate training scheme, designed for their recruits from university, but I was allowed to join as a customer's son. I spent most of the time working in a factory in Street, Somerset, where I was useless at every practical task, but when we were due to be taught about Time and Motion (the latest technique spreading through all the Clarks factories) I was excluded in case I learnt something that could be used to advantage in the Timpson factory at Kettering (I would have been of no help).

As a consequence I spent the six weeks before Christmas working in the Peter Lord shop in the centre of Sheffield. It was so cold in my digs, on most mornings the glass of water by my bed was frozen.

There were four Timpson shoe shops in the centre of Sheffield, the busiest achieving six times the turnover of Peter Lord. I started to see why they mainly made shoes and we sold them. In the 1960s Clarks weren't particularly good at shopkeeping but had such a strong brand they would only supply retailers who stuck to the rules. Clarks arrogantly insisted that no one could stock their brand unless they supplied a 'minimum presence'. Which meant sizes and half sizes in so many lines there was little space on the fixtures for any other brand.

Their biggest customers, Milwards, Charles Clinkard and John Farmer, all better retailers than Peter Lord, were able to prosper despite the Clarks package of high stocks and low margins.

When I did my graduate course at Street, Clarks was still very much a family business with Anthony Clark and his cousin Peter Clothier in charge, and Lance Clark soon to become chief executive. But Lance was the fifth generation and, with lots of cousins and second cousins all holding a piece of the equity, life was never going to be easy. Lance is probably the most unconventional chief executive I've met. One autumn he arrived to address a Timpson meeting in Edinburgh and launch a new Timpson/Clark initiative, but when it was his time to speak he'd disappeared to go round an art gallery. Lance once came to my office with his arm in a sling. He'd just returned from a trip on the Trans-Siberian railway. En route he met a Latvian who challenged Lance to a bout of wrestling. They fought on the platform at their next stop and Lance broke his arm. Despite all these eccentricities Clarks fought off a shareholder battle, resisting demands to go public, and is still in private hands with a substantial slice of the retail shoe market.

*

One branded multiple survives alongside Clarks. Charles Clinkard, founded and still run in the North-East by the Clinkard family, are the mature customer's branded equivalent of Russell & Bromley. Founded in 1924, they now have 33 shops.

Startrite has always given Clarks some competition for

the children's fitting shoe trade and there were other branded retailers including Lotus and Norvic, but the major rival to Peter Lord was K Shoes – much better retailers than Peter Lord – run in the 1970s by another eccentric, George Probert, under the Chairmanship of Spencer Crookenden.

Once Clarks had bought K Shoes and moved the whole operation, including George Probert, down to Somerset there was only one major force left in the world of branded shoe retailing.

From about 1977 we were part of a sales sharing scheme called Footwear Retail Statistics that anonymously compared your company's sales figures with fifteen others. Despite all the secrecy it seemed clear that one chain consistently, and for the rest of us, annoyingly, outperformed everyone else. The star performer was John Farmer.

John Farmer was another family business (a lot of the best retailers are) that was developed from their base in Aldershot. When I first met Patrick Farmer at a conference in 1976 I had no idea that we would get to know each other so well. In 1982, in order to pay death duties when their father died, Patrick and his brother Tim were forced to sell the business to United Drapery Stores where Timpson joined them as a fellow subsidiary a year later. It was now even more annoying that Patrick and Tim were always above me in the sales league, but with other UDS companies coming in with considerably worse figures we both survived until UDS was bought by Hanson Trust. The day that we completed our management buyout with Hanson I met Patrick and Tim at Rules restaurant for dinner with Roger Lane-Smith, the lawyer who had done our deal. He nearly did the same for Farmers – if it hadn't been for some pessimistic cash forecasting they might well have got their independence. In the event Philip Birch of Ward White came in with an unhelpfully big bid which was topped by Clarks, so from 1983 John Farmer was owned by Clarks.

Initially, apart from frequent visits to budget meetings in Street, Patrick and Tim were left alone to run the business. They were a perfect partnership, both a bit conservative and quick to see the possibility of trouble ahead, so, unlike most retailers, they were unlikely to be guilty of overtrading. But Tim was a clever buyer who knew his numbers and how to build a range, while Patrick was, and is, good at property and, even more important, the perfect people person who knew everyone in the business and they really liked knowing him.

Patrick and Tim did so well they were given more to do, taking control of other Clarks retail brands Rohan and Ravel, a fashion chain that can't have fitted into any sensible Clarks long-term business plan. Anyone at Street with any sense would have seen the point of putting all Clarks retail under Farmer management, but business is not always simply about common sense and putting the best team in to bat. Company politics also have a part to play and about this time Street was swarming with office politicians.

The management of Ravel was transferred to a team in Street and soon withered, while Farmers were absorbed into Peter Lord, together with Milwards, a sleepy Reading-based acquisition which used to stock mainly Clarks shoes in about twenty shops run by the family, with a strong Christian ethic. Patrick was put on the main board with responsibility for Clarks Overseas. Three years later, in his mid-fifties, Patrick retired – bad news for Clarks but great news for Timpson.

That is how we were able to recruit Patrick Farmer, probably the most complete retailer I have ever known, as a non-executive director.

THE TAILORS FROM LEEDS
AND LIFE WITH THE LYONS

Joseph Hepworth, Henry Price, Montague Burton and the Lyons family, who together created the biggest names in multiple tailoring, all built their businesses from offices and factories based in Leeds.

For most of the twentieth century a basic part of nearly every man's wardrobe was a two- or three-piece suit for best. They all needed a suit for weddings, funerals, Saturday nights and church on Sunday. Look at old holiday pictures and you will even see some men wearing a suit on the beach. Today we still expect suits to be worn at weddings and funerals, and many young men wear a suit to go horseracing (check out Ladies' Day at Aintree) but suits are bought off the peg, ready to wear. Before 1975 most suits were made to measure.

Hepworth, Burtons, Fifty Shilling Tailors and Alexandre together with many other names including Willoughby and Weaver to Wearer all had their own factories, mostly in Leeds, aiming to provide a ten day service to shops all over the country.

The shops had lots of display but little stock. At least half the ground floor was given over to enormous windows which were meticulously merchandised to show off the range of styles and colours with the cheapest, bestselling, styles at the front of the window.

Samples of all the available cloths were displayed in books on a table in the middle of the spacious lobby where the top salesman hovered, waiting to pounce on any prospective customer. A successful sales assistant could double his (they were nearly all men) fairly paltry basic pay by earning commission. Their technique was to engage the innocent window shopper in casual conversation (like a modern day charity chugger) and persuade their prey to walk inside, look at the range of styles, and pick a pattern, preferably from the high price range or a discontinued cloth that carried the highest commission rate. Once the customer agreed to be measured, the sale was all but certain. After 30 minutes making decisions about style and material and having a tape measure run across the shoulder blades and the inside leg checked, most people were only too happy to hand over a deposit, sign the order form agreeing to the credit terms (no one talked APR in those days) and get out of the shop. Things did not always go so smoothly when the customer returned ten days later for a fitting. Assuming the completed suit had made it back to the shop, there was no certainty that it would fit. The shop staff blamed the factory for failing to follow instructions and the factory blamed the sales assistant for faulty measurement; every branch needed an onsite tailor to make a few quick alterations. But as the customer probably desperately needed the suit for that weekend, a suit that just sort of fitted was better than no suit at all.

*

Joseph Hepworth developed his business several decades before his big rivals. He started in Leeds in 1864 and twenty years later had 100 shops serviced by a factory with 500 employees. This was well before Montague Burton, at the age of 18, in 1903, borrowed £100 to open an outfitter's shop in Chesterfield. Ten years later he had five shops around Sheffield and a factory based in Leeds. By 1929 the chain had grown to 400 shops backed by the biggest clothing factory in Europe. Burton took a big interest in property, putting up new buildings on freehold sites, often with a billiard hall above the shop. If you look carefully above some of their old shops you can still see the Burton logo carved into the stonework. When Montague Burton died in 1952 his company had 616 shops and claimed to be the largest multiple tailor in the world.

Henry Price started his tailoring business just after Burton, in 1905. His company was called Prices Tailors and, perhaps using his surname as a prompt to offer the best value for money, he advertised his low prices on the fascia by calling the chain 'Thirty Shilling Tailors', a name that was later changed to 'Fifty Shilling Tailors' – making the clear promise that they could supply a suit for less than £2/10/0d (£2.50) which probably translates to about £70 in today's money.

Alexandre, another Leeds-based made-to-measure tailor, was developed by the Lyons family who in 1955 sold out to United Drapery Stores, an acquisitive group that owned about 250 stores including Claude Alexander, a tailoring business with all its branches in Scotland. It was really a reverse takeover because two second-generation Lyons brothers took over the management of United Drapery Stores: Bernard, as chairman, ran the tailoring side, while his brother Jack got stuck into the stores. Within a year of the United Drapery deal Bernard had bought Prices Tailors who by then had 350 shops. No doubt dubious about the Fifty Shilling brand name and all the restrictions it could bring, the shops were renamed 'John Collier' and Bernard set about running all three brands,

John Collier, Alexandre Ltd and Claude Alexander, from one central office in Leeds. Bernard was brilliantly successful. Although the Fifty Shilling name disappeared John Collier still kept a reputation for value, while both Alexandre and Claude Alexander benefited from the economies of scale that came with a chain of over 600 shops. Bernard Lyons was beating Burtons at every turn. Better prices, quicker service, more fashionable styling and memorable advertising: 'John Collier, John Collier, the Window to Watch'. Bernard paid a lot of attention to detail, insisting that there was a smart sales assistant standing by the pattern table in every lobby and making sure the windows followed company display instruction to the letter. He even made sure every shop started their sale ten days before Christmas (the day after last orders could be placed for Christmas delivery).

Bernard had one major move left to make. He made a bid to buy Burton which would have given him a chain of well over a thousand shops and made United Drapery Stores the biggest retailer in the UK. Bernard was thwarted by the Monopolies and Mergers Commission and although UDS Tailoring (as he called John Collier, Alexandre and Claude Alexander) continued to do well, United Drapery Stores (renamed UDS) had to look beyond menswear for other businesses to buy.

With UDS already controlling a number of department stores it made sense for the Lyons to add new stores to their portfolio which by the 1960s had collected a number of well-known names including Whiteleys of Bayswater, Arding & Hobbs of Clapham, Landport of Portsmouth, Macross in Cardiff and Allders of Croydon which became the country's third biggest store after Selfridges and Harrods.

But with their tailoring experience the Lyons felt more

comfortable with multiple retailing and made a particular success out of the clothing chain Richard Shops which had great retail sites and a strong following from smart women looking for pretty clothes at value prices.

They probably bought the fur chain Swears & Wells from its founding Ross family to acquire some valuable freeholds, especially two in Oxford Street, London. After a few years of property deals and shop closures the remaining 30 Swears & Wells units were combined with another acquisition, the Liverpool-based Suede Centre whose founder stayed on to run the Swears & Wells/Suede Centre subsidiary. Other UDS companies included the Blundell Credit Company, John Myers Home Shopping (mail order) and footwear retailer Farmers.

*

We, at Timpson, were next. Following a board room row that finished in my father being fired as chairman, we looked for someone to buy our family shareholding and in 1972 found Bernard Lyons.

As I was surrounded by directors who were on the opposite side of our internal feud the Lyons took pity and found me a minor role at John Collier, as their shoe buyer. I arrived at the Leeds head office on the day they were celebrating a record week for sales. They were cock-a-hoop, beating Burton to bits and giving much better value than Hepworth.

My job was unrewarding. I was only allowed to put shoes into twenty shops and display them on the first floor – no one was allowed to invade the space occupied by the made-to-measure salesmen on the ground floor.

What struck me, as I was visiting the few shops that were allowed to stock my shoes, was the lost opportunity. Shops that sold 150 suits a week sold fewer than ten shirts; it didn't seem right when Marks & Spencer provided a complete wardrobe and were selling more suits and shirts every year.

The record week didn't help. What could be wrong with a business that was performing at the top of the chart? The Lyons had a winning formula but the market was changing and they were stuck in the past. Multiple tailors were about to be yesterday's men.

My second meeting with Bernard Lyons was an unexpectedly lucky encounter. I had gone to London to hand in my resignation. During four months of buying shoes for John Collier I spent much of the time gardening and playing golf. I turned down the offer of buying boys' shoes for John Myers Home Shopping and wasn't tempted by an invitation to be an assistant shoe buyer at Whiteleys department store in Bayswater. It was time for me to find my happiness elsewhere.

Before I could blurt out my resignation, Bernard Lyons asked me a strange question: 'Do you live anywhere near Liverpool?' I told him I did. 'We have a business there called Swears & Wells and most of the management had to go. Can you go there and run it until we can find a proper managing director?' I started a week on Monday.

It was my lucky break and I lasted in the job for nearly two years until I was asked to return and run the Timpson business, where the first job was to close 120 shops branded Norvic which Timpson bought a year before we sold to UDS. It was good training.

I quickly learnt what I called groupmanship – how to survive while running a subsidiary within a big group. The rules are simple: 'Make sure at least one other company in the group is doing worse than you are!'

I handed over the running of Swears & Wells to Jack Maxwell who was chief executive of Richard Shops, top performer in the UDS league, but it was unfortunate timing. Richard Shops suddenly found sales hard to come by and Maxwell needed Swears & Wells like a hole in the head.

Following the experience gained closing Norvic I was wheeled out to organise the Swears & Wells closing down sale.

The first really bad bit of UDS news came from John Myers Home Shopping which suddenly produced a mammoth loss and was rescued by Great Universal Stores in a very distressed sale.

UDS persuaded shareholders to subscribe for a rights issue and spent most of the proceeds on the fashion chain Van Allan. I'm not sure how the acquisition fitted into the UDS plan, if they had one, but it was certainly money badly spent. Within three years of the purchase Jack Maxwell, who took responsibility for Van Allan alongside Richard Shops, turned up at the Van Allan head office at Enderby near Leicester to announce the chain was closing down. 'It's been a bad week for both of us', he said to an incredulous team facing redundancy, 'yesterday one of my racehorses broke a leg and had to be put down.' I was asked to help with the Van Allan closing down sale.

I never had much problem meeting my groupmanship target. UDS Tailoring sales fell as they were slow to introduce a full range of ready-to-wear merchandise. They still thought there was a big business in made-to-measure. Richard Shops was making less money and the only star performers were Farmers, who always did well, and the Duty Free business that was being developed at Heathrow and Gatwick.

It couldn't last. The comfort I got by being surrounded by poor performing retailers was bound to end in tears. After a number of profit warnings UDS was bandied about as a take-over target and eventually in 1983 became part of Hanson Trust, a serial asset-stripper.

Most of the different UDS management teams tried to achieve a management buyout and Hanson started to sell off parts of UDS in September 1983. Luckily we were successful; Farmers nearly made it but finished up in the hands of Clarks, their major supplier; Richard Shops were within hours of doing a deal but finally finished as part of Terence Conran's Storehouse empire. Hanson made it clear that Allders was not for sale but changed their mind three years later when Finance Director Harvey Lipsith did a deal. The UDS Tailoring team led by Managing Director David Hall completed a buyout, but it didn't last. Within eighteen months the shops were sold to Burtons and the John Collier fascia disappeared.

In 1950 every town had a number of made-to-measure tailors that were recognised as being the most profitable retailers on the high street. Today, no mass multiple makes suits to measure and Burton is the only tailoring name still trading (although it is a shadow of the Burton that became the biggest tailor in the world).

Every successful retailer must never forget that nothing is for ever, today's category killer can become tomorrow's favourite for administration. Every retailer needs to look at least ten years ahead.

JOHN LEWIS PARTNERSHIP

When I was in my twenties I was given two strong hints that John Lewis was a special sort of business. First, a nurse called Juliet, who was one of my sister's best friends, got a job in Nottingham working for Jessops, a John Lewis store in the city centre. I knew about Jessops because Mrs Fowler shopped there (she was my landlady when I lived in digs at West Bridgford while a student at Nottingham University). But I couldn't understand why a fully qualified nurse with a really caring attitude would want to give it all up to become a shop assistant. It was some time before I discovered that she was still a nurse, playing her part in the welfare team that looked after the Partners working at Jessops.

A few years later I met Di, wife of Kit Green, who had just joined Timpson as our Marketing Manager (in the days when we had a Marketing Department). Di, a John Lewis graduate trainee, was a huge fan of the Partnership, particularly the way they dealt with personnel and training. Being a northerner, many miles away from Peter Jones or the nearest Waitrose, I was unaware that to many the John Lewis Partnership had become a very special business. I was about to learn the importance of creating a caring company culture.

The enlightened attitude towards employees, which has become a hallmark of the way John Lewis does business, was far from present in the original store on Oxford Street, London where the sales assistants, like most in the retail trade at that time, worked long hours for a low rate of pay. The business was founded in 1864 after John Lewis, who was brought up near Shepton Mallet in Somerset, moved from a promising career with Peter Robinson to open a haberdashery store nearby in modest premises at 132 Oxford Street. He built the business by gradually acquiring adjacent buildings and widening his range of merchandise, but always offering good quality and taking a low margin.

John Lewis gave 25 per cent of the equity to each of his two sons John Spedan and Oswald, expecting both of them to help to run the business. Oswald didn't particularly enjoy retailing so he sold the shares back to his father to pursue a career in politics. As the business ultimately discovered, it can be quite a good thing if just one member from each generation emerges as the clear leader of the family business.

The founder, John Lewis, made a major move when he bought the impressive-looking but loss-making Peter Jones department store on Sloane Square for £20,000 in 1906. For several years this new acquisition didn't make any money until John Lewis put his son in charge.

John Spedan Lewis followed his father's principles of good quality, low margins and great customer service but he added a new dimension. He felt that the employees were overworked, underpaid and lacked the recognition they deserved. He wanted to pay lower dividends to shareholders and give his employees the chance to share in success.

Unlike other retailers John Spedan realised that happy contented sales assistants would give a better service. He thought his staff should be supported and encouraged. He introduced shorter hours and a sales commission as well as keeping members informed about company plans and listening to individual points of view. It made a difference; as staff felt more valued the performance at Peter Jones improved. This was in stark contrast to the experience in the John Lewis store in Oxford Street where the founder followed the traditional hard line with employees. For a time father and son went in opposite directions, John Lewis keeping to his strict regime in Oxford Street while son John Spedan introduced more staff-centred policies at Peter Jones on Sloane Square. He increased holidays to three weeks, set up a staff council and produced a regular newsletter, later renamed *The Gazette*. Next, he paid part of the dividends to staff and started calling them Partners. Eventually the father recognised the wisdom of his son's management style, the two stores became part of one business and John Spedan provided further benefits to his 'Partners' including free holiday accommodation in company-owned hotels. When his father died John Spedan bought the shares his brother Oswald had inherited and became owner of 100 per cent of the business. Now in total control, he was able to take his belief in employee involvement a stage further, by handing over his shareholding to a trust that was established for the John Lewis Partners.

John Spedan Lewis not only established a strong culture, he also took some strategic decisions that laid the foundation for future success. He captured his merchandising policy in one phrase 'Never Knowingly Undersold', a simple way of advertising both good value and competitiveness, which is now copied by supermarkets that promise to 'price match' their rivals.

In the 1930s the company grew well beyond the two central London stores with the acquisition of single stores like Jessops, my landlady's favourite and, of great significance many years later, he purchased ten grocery shops called Waitrose. In 1940 the business got a lot bigger by buying all the sixteen Selfridges Provincial Stores which included George Henry Lee in Liverpool, Robert Sayle in Cambridge and Trewin Brothers in Watford.

John Spedan Lewis had an unusual and successful style which put the Partners at the centre of his thinking. The Trust he established for the Partners gave them ownership of the business and a say in the way it is run, but for that relationship to work the Partnership needed successive generations of management who saw things in the same way.

John Spedan's son, Edward, was not keen to join the business but his nephew Peter, Oswald's son, carried on the family tradition. Despite their success the family couldn't have imagined that the Partnership principles would still be the central strength of the business 150 years after John Lewis opened his store in Oxford Street, with the culture now being put into practice by business leaders who aren't members of the family.

*

Andy Street, who became managing director of John Lewis in 2007, has spent all his working life with the Partnership after graduating from Oxford in 1985. He has provided the Partnership with a perfect management package. He totally gets the culture, understands how to motivate the Partners and has shown a sure-footed strategic instinct that has kept the Partnership up to date and ahead of the competition. Andy Street comes across as a clear thinker who runs the business by common sense. He works for and on behalf of the Partners but that doesn't stop him taking tough decisions. As the top guy at John Lewis he is responsible for strategy. He listens a lot and discusses his plans before making a major decision. But far from handing all the power over to the Partners, Andy Street takes full responsibility for the strategy: the buck stops at his desk.

The difference between Andy Street and most bosses is that he is working for his employees – the Partners as shareholders have the final say on whether he keeps his job.

The structure has helped the business take a long-term view. In 2008, when the recession first hit the high street, most retailers cut prices to keep up turnover and cut back on capital expenditure to preserve the cash. They all had one eye on their institutional shareholders who were quick to criticise a poor like-for-like sales performance. In contrast John Lewis stuck to their long-term plans and produced a much poorer sales performance than their competitors in the run-up to Christmas 2008. Two years later, thanks to keeping their cool, they were increasing market share at a proper margin.

Andy Street has consistently stuck to a sure-footed strategy which has kept the company up to date, but he keeps to the old Partnership principles, recognising that a strong culture is a company's greatest asset. He understands that it takes a long time to build a reputation. His adventurous management style has never been allowed to compromise the company culture.

The talented top team have adapted to a changing market while keeping faith with the culture which is the central source of success.

*

John Spedan Lewis would have been pretty proud to have seen how John Lewis has used his partnership model to create the most successful department store chain in the UK, but he would have been amazed to discover that the Partnership also has, in Waitrose, a leading and fast-growing chain of supermarkets.

The Partnership took full advantage of the Waitrose acquisition. The ten shops purchased in 1937 led to a chain of supermarkets that catered for the John Lewis customer – in this case the 'Never Knowingly Undersold' promise led to innovative own-branded food with high quality at value prices. Not the cheapest, but the preferred choice of shoppers who could afford the best.

By 2007, when Mark Price became managing director (his appointment was made in the same year Andy Street took charge of the department stores) there were 183 Waitrose stores but hardly any north of Watford (the most northerly was in Newark).

While Andy Street was quietly keeping the John Lewis chain up to date Mark Price turned Waitrose into a national chain. The Morrisons bid for Safeway led to a number of disposals, forced by the competition authorities, and Waitrose suddenly started to appear as far north as Sandbach. With further deals that brought Waitrose stores from Somerfield, the Co-operative Group and Woolworths, within six years the chain had nearly doubled in size to 300 stores. The business is still largely based in the South of England (particularly the South-East) but you can now find a Waitrose in Jesmond, north of Newcastle, and Morningside, a suburb of Edinburgh. Despite the rapid growth, the Partnership still has plenty of scope with lots of communities keen to be given the opportunity to shop at Waitrose.

Mark Price, who has been pursuing his career in parallel to Andy Street, has faced a different challenge. At Waitrose he has been using the foundation of the Partnership principles to create a new business. Unlike his supermarket rivals, who are often cast in the role of an evil giant, Price has managed to put Waitrose on a bit of a pedestal by being seen to look after colleagues, customers and the surrounding community.

Mark Price and Andy Street have provided the Partnership with two equally strong businesses, both with the potential to grow much bigger. The Partnership principles created by John Spedan Lewis have provided both Price and Street with a unique advantage over their competitors, but both men have, in return, done a great job on behalf of the Partners. Peter Jones is still the flagship and the only store to keep its original name (apart, of course, from the John Lewis store on Oxford Street). All the provincial stores acquired over the years with their loyal band of local customers, including Bainbridge in Newcastle, Heelas in Reading and Mrs Fowler's favourite Jessops in Nottingham, were renamed John Lewis. Other department store groups like House of Fraser, Allders and Debenhams struggled to keep an old-fashioned portfolio up to date but John Lewis put investment into newly built stores linked to the latest city centre and out-of-town precincts. This ability to think one step ahead has also helped John Lewis to prosper from internet shopping with an emphasis on Click and Collect, proving that department stores can still be on the leading edge of retailing.

TRADITIONAL DEPARTMENT STORES

I've already mentioned my mother taking me shopping to Mr Hulme the butcher who seemed to know every customer in Hale Barns and always gave me sweets, and the smell of coffee in Cadman's the grocer in Hale where everything was packed in brown paper bags, but my most vivid memories are of our visits to Kendal Milne, the department store on both sides of Deansgate, Manchester where I was expected to be on my best behaviour. Department stores were the retail aristocrats, proper shopkeepers with doormen to greet you and the lift had a uniformed operator who announced the departments on every floor. I went to Kendal's for my first meeting with Father Christmas and to be fitted for the uniform when I went away to school. Every town had a department store and cities had several, with wonderful names like Hills of Hove, Pettigrew and Steven in Glasgow, Swan & Edgar in London, and Snowball & Son, which was known in Gateshead as the Harrods of the North.

Many of these traditional stores may have been similar to Grace Brothers, the fictitious setting for the television comedy *Are You Being Served?*, with floor walkers and a pecking order that let the longest-serving assistants serve almost every customer and earn most of the commission.

I got a glimpse of the past when we acquired a shoe repair concession in Chadds of Lowestoft. It was 1990 but little at

Chadds had changed, as I learnt during a branch visit when I was summoned into the chairman's office to have tea with the 80-year-old Mr Chadd. He was charming and chatted about the good old days when customer service was king, sales assistants started on £3.3.6d (£3.18) a week and Chadds was the focal point of Lowestoft. He was still proud of the store although it was clearly struggling. Like many department stores, Chadds found it hard to keep their traditions up to date during a time when Lowestoft lost a lot of its sparkle.

Chadds still exists but now trades as Palmers, a local department store group that bought the Lowestoft store in 2004. Palmers is one of an elite group of department store survivors, started in Great Yarmouth in 1837 (like many department stores as a small drapery shop) and after surviving two fires and bomb damage the original store now claims to be the longest established independent department store in the country.

Any company that has survived since 1837 deserves admiration. Many department stores were helped by owning their own freehold property but all had to create enough cash to fund big stock levels, high maintenance and regular refurbishment. I have already singled out the John Lewis Partnership as my pick of the store groups, but many others have built enduring businesses on the back of a small drapery store that got considerably bigger.

*

Although there is plenty of fiction among the facts used to create the television series *Mr Selfridge*, Harry Selfridge was a relative newcomer to the family founders of department stores, opening his Oxford Street store in 1909, but unlike most others, instead of starting with a little drapers that got much bigger, he built the major store of his dreams from scratch. It was a bold move by a courageous entrepreneur whose innovative window displays, special promotions, topical events and showmanship made shopping fun and set a standard for other stores to follow. If the definition of a great retailer is someone who has an outstanding talent for customer service, Harry Selfridge has to be a leading candidate. He expressed his personality in the store layout, his advertising and the way he recognised the role played by his shop staff.

In 1926 Selfridges started expanding by opening sixteen provincial stores but a combination of the 1929 Recession, increasing gambling debts, a lavish social life and business borrowings put Harry Selfridge under pressure. The bankers controlled his destiny. In 1941, six years before his death at the age of 89, he was ousted by the Selfridges Board.

The genius of Harry Selfridge wasn't emulated by his successors and during the 1940s the provincial stores became part of the John Lewis Partnership. In 1951 the Oxford Street store was bought by the Liverpool-based Lewis's store chain, which fourteen years later became part of Charles Clore's Sears Group. When Sears was in crisis in 1998 they demerged Selfridges, which in independent hands opened two stores in Manchester and one in Birmingham before being acquired by the present owner Garfield Weston.

*

Takeovers and rationalisation have constantly changed the shape of UK department stores, so it is not surprising that the biggest store chain today is the one that has gobbled up most of their competitors – Debenhams.

Debenhams' origin can be traced back to a drapery store in Wigmore Street, London in 1778 although William Debenham didn't become a partner until 1813. Descendant Ernest Debenham grew the business through a series of acquisitions in the early 20th century which included Harvey Nicholls in Knightsbridge, Marshall & Snellgrove in Oxford Street, Affleck & Brown in Manchester, Swan & Edgar on Piccadilly Circus, and Pauldens trading in both Sheffield and Manchester.

After the short time that Debenhams was part of the Burton Group, Harvey Nichols was sold to Dickson Poon in 1991 and the remaining stores were demerged, before Debenhams subsequently bought more stores from the failing Allders.

In some ways it is a pity that the old names have disappeared and been replaced by a national brand. One store, Browns of Chester, was allowed to keep its own well-trusted brand for many years but now even that has been changed to Debenhams.

A lot of the other family-run department stores have finished up as part of House of Fraser, which was itself a family business for four generations, starting with Hugh Fraser who opened a store on the corner of Buchanan Street and Argyle Street in Glasgow in 1849 under the name Arthur & Fraser. His son, grandson and great-grandson were all called Hugh and all ran the business, which bought many well-known stores including Arnott & Co and Binns, but the most significant acquisition was Harrods, which was purchased in 1959 and brought with it many other well-known names.

Charles Henry Harrod opened his first shop in 1824 on Borough High Street, Southwark. He was, like most department store pioneers, a draper, but had also opened a grocers in Clerkenwell before deciding to move to a small shop on Brompton Road.

It was the founder's son, Charles Digby Harrod, who really built the business. When he started in 1861 there were two assistants and a messenger boy. By 1880 he employed 100 people. Three years later when a fire all but gutted the store Charles Harrod used the disaster as an opportunity to rebuild a grander store before he retired in 1889 and floated the company.

The massive Harrods store we see today was finally opened in 1905 and having established the biggest shop in Britain, Harrods started buying some of its major competitors including Dickins & Jones, DH Evans, Kendal Milne, Swan & Edgar and Rackhams.

After a major takeover battle in 1959, House of Fraser beat Debenhams and United Drapery Stores to acquire Harrods. House of Fraser was now established as the UK's major store group and, under the chairmanship of Sir Hugh Fraser, continued to expand by buying about 50 more stores including Dingles and Army & Navy before considering a merger with Boots the Chemist.

Both Debenhams and House of Fraser found that buying up a large collection of department stores could cause considerable problems. Building maintenance is costly and regular refits are essential to keep the stores up to date. Some simply suffered as a result of redevelopment schemes that put an originally prime spot out of position. As a consequence both Debenhams and particularly House of Fraser had a number of poor-performing stores that looked sadly out of date.

The acquisitive House of Fraser suddenly looked vulnerable and they themselves became a target when in 1981 Lonrho launched a bid fiercely fought off by Sir Hugh Fraser's successor as chairman, Professor Roland Smith, who was helped by a reference to the Monopolies and Mergers Commission. The bid was defeated but had put House of Fraser on the defensive and four years after the Lonrho bid the company was purchased by the Al Fayed family. As a private company the Al Fayeds were able to rationalise the portfolio, closing the weakest stores, refurbishing those with good prospects and opening new stores connected to Meadowhall and Lakeside shopping centres.

In 1994 House of Fraser was relisted on the stock market, but not before Harrods had been hived off to become the Al Fayeds' trophy asset until it was sold in 2010 to Qatar Holdings.

For the next twenty years House of Fraser became more involved in corporate activity than store development. A number of old stores were closed, including Barkers in Kensington, Dickins & Jones and several stores in Scotland and Northern England. A hostile bid from Tom Hunter was followed by a successful approach from a consortium which has recently sold to Chinese retailer Nanjing Xinjiekou. Customers who have stayed loyal to the old stores like Howells in Cardiff and Hammonds of Hull that now trade as House of Fraser have seen their store pass through the hands of a lot of different management teams.

*

My personal involvement in department stores was during my time working for UDS Group who built up their own collection of traditional stores including Arding & Hobbs, Landports in Portsmouth, Mackross of Cardiff, Shinners of Sutton, Hinds of Eltham, Pages of Camberley and their two enormous stores Whiteleys in Bayswater and Allders of Croydon.

In my first few months after UDS had taken over Timpson I was offered a job at Whiteleys as a shoe buyer but quickly turned down the opportunity. The idea of working in an old-fashioned London store with long-serving floor managers and a traditional system of command and control filled me with horror.

But I couldn't totally escape. Two years later I was running the Timpson business with a shoe repair concession in every store, with each store manager convinced that he knew more about how to run a shoe repair business than we did. Our cause was not helped when UDS chairman, Bernard Lyons, sent his chauffeur into Whiteleys with his favourite crocodile shoes and we lost them.

Before UDS was taken over by Hanson in 1983 Whiteleys had already been closed and sold to developers who converted the store into a shopping centre. But the rest of the UDS stores continued under Hanson ownership for three years before being sold to a management buyout team led by former Hanson executive Harvey Lipsith.

The new business traded as Allders, converting all the stores to the name of the most successful store in the chain. The store in Croydon built up by Joshua Allder in the late 19th century was the third biggest store in the UK after Harrods and Selfridges. The buyout team traded for over ten years and opened more stores, but eventually finished in failure. Some stores went to Debenhams and House of Fraser but the third biggest store in the UK, Allders of Croydon, is now closed.

*

Most department stores started as small drapers, became a big family-owned store and were eventually acquired by one of the chains and the family name disappeared. Fenwicks has gone down a different route.

The business was started in Newcastle by John James (J.J.) Fenwick in 1882 and, apart from shrewdly buying a freehold in Bond Street, London in 1891, concentrated on developing the biggest and best store in Newcastle. This single-minded approach was helped by a poor experience in nearby Sunderland where a store opened in 1881 was closed a year later.

It has always been a family business, owned and run by the family: Fred Fenwick, then John followed by Mark. Eventually stores were opened in York, Windsor and Brent Cross and in 2001 the company made a major move by buying Bentalls with a magnificent store in Kingston, and Beales, but the poor-performing parts of these acquisitions were sold off and Fenwicks today has only eleven stores, a focused business with a consistent track record.

Department stores have come in all shapes and sizes and although the old 'Grace Brothers' store is part of history, Selfridges, Harrods, John Lewis and Fenwicks show that stores still have a big part to play on the modern high street.

BOOTS AND W.H. SMITH

A couple of nationwide chains which most people use on a regular basis have recently, in my opinion, both lacked buzz. They are shops where you feel the heavy hand of head office: Boots and W.H. Smith.

My judgement may have been biased by some unhappy experiences of poor service. One Friday three years ago in Newcastle-under-Lyme I wanted to buy the *Racing Post* to check details of two horses my wife Alex had running that day. While waiting in the checkout queue at Smith's I read everything I needed to know about the going, recent form, likely opposition and forecasts from all the expert tipsters. There were still seven people waiting in front of me when I put the paper back on display. Recently I had a similar experience in the Walsall branch of Boots where I was faced with another long queue for the checkout. I didn't have the ten minutes needed to pay so on this occasion I simply abandoned the merchandise on a nearby shelf.

Wage cost ratios driven by head office had been cut by inconveniencing customers, but I wondered whether these companies always had a cost-driven culture or if recent management has abandoned the principles on which their business had been built.

Shortly before he died in 1792, Henry Walton Smith

developed a newspaper round near Berkeley Square. His son William Henry, who was born just two weeks after his father's untimely death, also went into the news trade using the mail coach system to create a nationwide newspaper distribution network.

William Henry's son, who with a distinct lack of imagination was also called William Henry Smith, really got W.H. Smith off the ground when he took his father's newspaper network and put it on the railways. By building a good relationship with all the main railway companies he created a genuinely national network.

In 1848 he opened his first news stand at Euston, stocking not just newspapers but also books. It was an instant success; passengers found it a lot easier to read on a train than a stagecoach. By 1860 Smith's bookstalls had appeared in all the mainline stations and many of the minor ones. The younger William Henry had standards. In contrast to some of the disreputable publications sold by other station-based vendors, Smith vetted every publication before it could be offered for sale in his shops.

Smith wasn't just a businessman, he was also a politician and in 1868 was elected as a member of Parliament and six years later became First Lord of the Admiralty. He left the running of the family business to a barrister, William Lethridge, whom he had taken on as a partner.

After Smith's death in 1891 his widow was created Viscountess Hambleden, a title that on her death passed to her eldest son, who in 1913 became head of the business. W.H. Smith remained in the control of a family member until 1972, despite becoming a public company in 1949 (a necessary flotation to pay heavy death duties following the death of the third Viscount Hambleden).

Up to 1905 the company stuck to station bookstalls but a dispute over rent reviews with Great Western and London and North Western Railways led to a lot of leases coming to an end. These units were quickly replaced by opening shops nearby, thus starting a chain of W.H. Smith shops on the high street.

For over a century of family management W.H. Smith stuck to running bookshops and selling newspapers but as soon as the chairmanship passed into the hands of outsiders W.H. Smith looked to diversify.

In its search for new areas of profitable growth the company tackled a wide range of different trades, starting in 1978 with Homecentres, which traded as Do it All, followed by the first W.H. Smith Travel agency. Under the Chairmanship of Simon Hornby the company branched out into cable and satellite television, purchased a chain called Paperchase as well as Our Price Music. Through a number of takeovers they established an office supplies division while acquiring a number of bookshop competitors including Sherratt & Hughes and Waterstones.

After twenty years of diversification the company spent much of the next decade selling off most of these peripheral businesses. When Kate Swann was appointed Group chief executive to a struggling business in 2003 she immediately went back to basics. Unprofitable music departments were closed and the company concentrated on opening new outlets at Airport Terminals and motorway service stations. Thanks to a heavy dose of cost control, as sales declined profits increased, but these economies contributed to lower standards of customer care and longer checkout queues (although they are seldom as long as those in the 100+ Post Office counters that opened in W.H. Smith stores). Although the threadbare carpets in unloved W.H. Smith outlets became a feature on the internet, Kate Swann did invest some money and spent it wisely by focusing on the W.H. Smith tradition of supplying travellers with something to read. It was natural for a company built on railway stations to develop a major presence in international airports.

W.H. Smith was blown off course by a desire to diversify but has now rediscovered that business travellers, commuters and holidaymakers like to read when they are on the move. I just hope the day will come when I don't have to queue. It is nerve wracking to stand around waiting to pay when you have a train or a plane to catch.

*

As an undergraduate at Nottingham University I learnt a little about the history of Boots the Chemist. The Trent Building where I sat my exams, and Florence Boot, the hall of residence that was home to some female students who I never had the courage to ask out, were named to recognise the influence and finance the Boot family provided to help establish a university in the city where their business was founded.

In the mid-19th century, 100 years before the National Health Service was born, going to the doctor was expensive and many people found it difficult to afford the medicines they were prescribed. Consequently there was a substantial demand for herbal cures. John Boot, an agricultural worker, opened a small herbalist store on Goose Gate Nottingham in 1849. The business started well and was flourishing when John Boot died in 1860. His widow Mary continued trading with the help of son Jesse, who was only ten years old. The business did well and when Jesse took over control in his twenties he looked to expand. He widened the range on sale to include household goods and set up a major plank for the future by introducing proprietary medicines. He emphasised his aim of providing cures at an affordable cost by using the slogan 'Health for a Shilling'.

With sales growing steadily Jesse moved into larger premises on Goose Gate and started expanding with further shops around Nottingham, then in 1884 he opened shops in Lincoln and Sheffield. By 1890 he had ten stores.

The range of merchandise and services was influenced by Jesse's wife Florence whom he first met on a convalescent visit to Jersey where her family were in the book trade. It was her influence that introduced Boots to picture framing and their Booklovers' Lending Libraries, a feature that was still operating in the Boots store in Railway Street, Altrincham in 1961 while I was working as a shoe shop assistant in the Timpson store next door. But Jesse Boot's most important innovation was the introduction of in-store pharmacists, providing a true value alternative to a trip to the doctor.

The expanding business was based on buying drugs in bulk so Boots could offer better value than the competition. In 1885 Jesse Boot went a step further when he started manufacturing in the first of a number of factories that Boots set up in and around Nottingham.

By 1893 Jesse Boot had 33 shops, seven years later the chain had risen to 180 and within another year the acquisition of a combined 60 stores trading as the Metropolitan Drug Company and the Southern Drug Company pushed Boots' coverage to 250 shops. Before the First World War the rapid expansion increased the number of branches to over 550, backed up by a well-developed distribution system and a substantial investment in manufacturing. He must have been a tough negotiator, but compared with other employers of his generation he did much to look after the welfare of his workers and, with his 'Health for a Shilling' slogan always at the back of his mind, he put a premium on customer care.

The boy who, at the age of ten, had helped his mother run a small herbal remedy shop in Nottingham had developed the best-known pharmaceutical company in the UK. From humble beginnings he became Sir Jesse Boot in 1909 and a baronet seven years later.

In 1920, when he was 70, and the country was struggling to recover from the effects of the First World War, Jesse Boot, suffering from arthritis and fearing for the future, sold the company to the United Drug Company of America.

His son John was never happy with the sale but Jesse had every reason to be worried. The American purchasers suffered during the stock market crash of 1929 and put Boots up for sale. Two years after Jesse Boot (now Lord Trent) died in 1931, Boots returned to UK ownership and family control following an early form of management buyout. John Boot, the second Lord Trent, ran the business with an uncompromising authoritarian style for twenty years from 1933 to 1953, during which time he took the company well past 1,000 shops and built a pharmaceutical manufacturing capability of nationwide importance.

The Boots shops I remember in the late 1950s were pretty austere: wooden floors, old-fashioned counter service and prim-looking assistants, but John Boot had kept his father's formula of quality and value while continuing to show a caring social conscience in the way he treated employees. During his stewardship the second Lord Trent strengthened the manufacturing side and brought a significant addition to the merchandise range with the development of Boots No 7 cosmetics and the Soltan range of sunscreen products.

The tired-looking Boots chain received the boost it needed in 1967 with the acquisition of Timothy Whites & Taylors, a 622-outlet competitor with big shops that forced Boots into updating its retail format.

By the 1970s Boots had shops on nearly every shopping street. There was nowhere else to go, so it isn't surprising that successive professional management teams looked for ways to diversify.

I wonder what Jesse Boot would think about what has happened to Boots over the last 50 years. He certainly created plenty of potential to play acquisition games, both in the world of pharmaceutical research and production as well as on the high street.

The Boots board provided merchant bankers with plenty to do.

Boots went overseas, and between 1983 and 1987 bought Optrex (a deal that led to Boots Opticians), considered a merger with Glaxo, bought the Farley baby food business and launched Children's World, a retail concept they sold to Mothercare. In 1989, as well as making the logical acquisition of another chemist, Underwoods, they paid £900m to buy Ward White, which owned Halfords plus the DIY chains Payless and FADs. Later Children's World, Halfords and the DIY business were sold.

All this corporate activity was overshadowed by the deals done since 2007 when Alliance Boots was formed by the merger of Boots with the European group Alliance UniChem. A year later the group was bought out in a private equity deal, leaving the company with an awful lot of debt and giving the former Alliance UniChem chief executive Stefano Pessina plenty of shares and management control. He found a magic exit by merging with USA-based Walgreens who subsequently exercised an option to take over the whole of the Boots business. As a consequence our Boots shops in the UK are to Walgreen what Asda is to Walmart.

The shop where Jesse Boot helped his mother, Mary, as a ten-year-old boy, is now an enormous enterprise, but would Jesse be happy if he had to queue at the checkout?

STANLEY KALMS

In 1963, while I was an undergraduate at Nottingham University, my father, as Chairman of Timpson, came to talk to the students. He described the pitfalls of footwear retailing (father was never an optimist) and when it came to questions my tutor asked, 'Why don't you sell cameras?' Dixons had just floated on the stock exchange and camera shops were the smart deal on the high street.

Stanley Kalms was in the right business, but he didn't stand still. Over his 55-year executive career he showed a remarkable ability to reinvent his shops and finish up in the right trade at the right time.

In 1937, Kalms's father Charles opened a photographic studio in Southend and picked the name Dixons out of a telephone directory because the shop had a small fascia so he needed a short name. Charles opened five more studios but most were closed during the Second World War and when Stanley joined his father in 1948, short of his seventeenth birthday, there was just one studio left, in Edgware.

Within two years Stanley started to sell cameras and had the vision of turning the business into 'toy shops for men'. It was a good time to go into the camera business. He became the camera buyer and went to the Far East to find great value and the latest technology. Sales grew, helped by local advertising which also created a mail order business, and by 1957 he had opened five new shops. In 1962, a year before my father spoke at Nottingham, Dixons was able to float. Stanley saw the stock market quote as the cue to be acquisitive, first buying camera competitors and then spreading his offer into the electrical business.

There seems little doubt that Stanley Kalms's sure touch came from his early experience. It is bound to help when the man at the top has business in his blood and started on the shop floor. He was a hands-on retailer doing business by walking round the office and visiting shops. He liked to listen to the gossip, left his office door wide open and wanted to be the first to know the sales and the latest news, especially the bad news. From all accounts he was a tough boss with a blunt way of getting his message across. If Dixons had a weakness it was their standard of customer service; perhaps the uncompromising management style influenced the way colleagues dealt with customers.

If customer care was an Achilles' heel, display and marketing was a masterclass. One feature we copied from Dixons is still used at Timpson today – we call the temporary sign we hang outside every one of our shops every day the 'Dixon Flag'. I was also always impressed with the way Dixons promoted the product in their Supasnaps photo processing subsidiary. Even more impressive was the deal they did with Sketchley who bought Supasnaps for £4.5m, with digital cameras just around the corner.

Kalms's big deal was buying Currys in 1984 after a bitter battle that ended with Kalms giving the Curry family management their cards on day one – more evidence of his blunt approach. The Currys deal put Dixons in a strong position, with most major competitors like Rumbelows and the Regional Electricity Boards proving to be fairly incompetent competition. Dixon became a runaway market leader.

Stanley Kalms didn't achieve this sure-footed navigation through the retail landscape on his own. From 1986 John Clare became part of a very successful double act that inevitably led to Clare becoming Kalms's successor as chief executive, a role he held for thirteen years until his retirement from Dixons in May 2007.

The next logical move met with disappointment when Dixon failed in their attempt to buy Kingfisher, owner of Woolworths and B&Q. A few years later Kingfisher also failed when they responded by trying to buy Dixons.

Towards the end of his executive career Stanley Kalms had an unexpected bonus – the speculative investment in web provider Freeserve proved to be a £1.5bn bonanza, but you wonder whether this was pure luck or simply good judgement. Perhaps it was further evidence that Stanley Kalms showed genius at moving at the right time to the right place.

When Kalms stepped down as chairman in 2001 and became Life President people wondered whether the business would miss his measured decision-making. Many saw signs of his absence when the group decided to change the Dixons fascia to Currys Digital. But the company came through the recession in good enough shape to merge with Carphone Warehouse and, despite having the Currys name on the fascias, the new company is called Dixons Carphone.

I can't help thinking that Kalms's sure touch is still helping to reinvent the business.

MOBILE PHONE SHOPS

For years it was almost impossible to find small high street shops at rents low enough for a cobbler to make a profit. We didn't need any more than 250 square feet but there always seemed to be other retailers, with new retail concepts, who could trade in tiny shops and were happy to expand their business by paying well over what we regarded as a reasonable rent.

In the early 1970s we were outbid by fast-growing new chains selling jeans. They were followed by a collection of niche retailers – Tie Rack and Sock Shop would pay particularly big rents for very small shops and the agents who were commissioned to spearhead their expansion were keen to fulfil their requirements list at any price. In the early 1990s we competed for sites with the new photo processing shops, Supasnaps, Max Spielmann, Snappy Snaps and Foto Processing. Whenever each new retail format found their market was saturated, another appeared to take their place and pay top rents for tiny shops. We never expected that our next big competitor would be selling mobile phones.

My grandchildren, who consider me, quite correctly, to be a technical dunce, were surprised to discover that I had a mobile phone in about 1980. It was a very heavy Motorola-branded big box that I found complicated to operate. On the rare occasions that I managed to make a connection the reception was seldom good enough for a conversation of more than a minute. In the 1980s it was difficult to envisage a country full of hand-held devices used by over 90 per cent of the population.

*

John Cauldwell was one of the few UK entrepreneurs who spotted the potential of the mobile phone market when he was working as a car salesman. In 1987 he set up his Midland Mobile Phone wholesale business which by 1991 had a turnover of £13m. He was dealing in devices similar to my original Motorola and, with phones selling for at least £2,000 each, it was a limited market. John Cauldwell was primarily a wholesaler who added a retail arm, Phones4U, which, perhaps conditioned by Cauldwell's time in the car showroom, was always seen to be the hard-sell player in the mobile market. Most mobile phone shops had little on display and although they sell physical phones they make most of the money from selling a service contract and any additional insurance. Phones4U saw the advantage of employing sharp sales assistants, who were often seen outside the shop plying for trade with any passing pedestrian. It was a slick operation that was driven by hard selling and it worked. John Cauldwell realised that he was operating in an ever-changing industry which was dominated by some very big IT businesses who themselves had entered the high street in direct competition to Phones4U.

In 2006, having ridden on the top of the mobile phone technical boom for nineteen years, Cauldwell shrewdly sold to private equity investors for £1.47bn. The retail business only survived for eight more years before it was squeezed out by big mobile network suppliers who were also Phones4U competitors. John Cauldwell did amazingly well to make so much money in a world dominated by multinational companies.

*

Apart from Richard Branson, who opened outlets to support Virgin Mobile, the other UK entrepreneur who was way ahead of other mobile thinkers was Charles Dunstone. He started selling mobile phones from his London flat in 1989 and a year later opened his first shop in Marylebone High Street, which reached sales of £1.2m in its first year, mainly from sales of Nokia 101 – a phone the size of a biggish brick which was just light enough to be called a mobile rather than a carphone. Dunstone called his shops Carphone Warehouse – at that time, the concept of a universal personal cellphone wasn't a realistic possibility.

Dunstone was joined in the business by his Uppingham school contemporary David Ross and as soon as it was clear they had stumbled on a winning formula the pair set about developing a chain of shops. (It isn't clear which of them was the inspiration behind the Carphone culture, and which drove the frenetic growth of shop openings.)

They not only spotted the potential of mobile technology but also understood what customers needed from a shop. Although the first purchasers tended to be 'techies' who were in love with all the latest technical gizmos, gradually Carphone Warehouse attracted customers who didn't understand what made them tick, they just wanted a portable phone that worked. As Dunstone observed, 'they're not much use to a customer who doesn't know how to switch it on.' Right from the start Carphone Warehouse colleagues were there to help customers, not just to sell to them.

If Dunstone had the initial ideas and understood the fundamental importance of customer service, David Ross clearly played an important part in pushing the pace of retail expansion both in the UK and in Europe. One bold move made a big difference: the acquisition in 1999 of Tandy, a loss-making electrical chain, more than doubled the number of UK stores from 180 to 450. When the Tandy fascia was changed and the shops converted, much larger shops started to trade under the Carphone Warehouse brand.

The Carphone Warehouse team worked out that to give customers the advice required, they needed special people working in their shops – intelligent people with personality. They were happy to pay much more than the normal, minimum, retail rate of pay to attract the A-level candidates and graduates they needed. They also discovered the benefits that come from selling long-term phone contracts which bring the certainty of rental income for several years to come.

If Charles Dunstone had been a born and bred retailer I doubt whether he would have taken the business in so many different directions. By 2005, Ross was becoming increasingly non-executive and eventually left the Board in 2008. Dunstone meanwhile, with the help of, among others, long-time Finance Director Roger Taylor, was thinking well outside the box by developing Talk Talk, his own internet service provider. It was a development that proved to be almost too successful when Dunstone advertised for new subscribers by offering Free Broadband. The response was so big it threatened to shut down his system and ruin his reputation.

Dunstone showed clear leadership and put the business back on track by admitting personal responsibility and taking the blame for a mistake that could have had fatal consequences for Carphone.

Although he made an error by setting up joint ventures with the major US electrical goods retailer Best Buy, he seems to have recovered with a well-timed merger with Dixon/Currys which got an early boost from the closure of Phones4U (Currys already collecting market share after Comet disappeared a year earlier). By acquisitions and mergers, Dunstone has put Carphone Warehouse (now Dixons Carphone) in a strong competitive place. His clear thinking, authority and vision make him seem to the IT world what Sir Michael Bishop of British Midland Airways was to the world of aviation or Lord Weinstock of GEC in electronics. By boldly backing his hunches and doing some well-timed deals Dunstone has created a powerful business that still relies heavily on its retail arm, which in turn relies on great people in each store providing a really helpful service.

Phones4U and Carphone Warehouse were built by entrepreneurs, but most of the phone shops that seem to occupy nearly half the shops on some streets have been developed by network providers as part of their marketing strategy. Apart from the branding there is little obvious difference between one brand and another. They are minimalist shops – a lot of plain walls with little merchandising. In truth they have a very small range of products to sell, but at least they are not as soulless as shops that sell e-cigarettes, and it's handy, when you have lost or forgotten the charger for your iPad or BlackBerry, to know there is bound to be a mobile phone shop nearby.

Either Charles Dunstone is very lucky or he has had an amazing vision in anticipating the way our digital world has developed. By basing his business around the mobile phone he entered a world of increasing opportunity. Surely he didn't know that the big device that he sold in his first shop would develop into the most used gadget in the world, which can take pictures, play music, become a television, be a navigator, pay bills and control all the appliances in your home.

Dunstone might not have known exactly what was coming next but when it arrived he took full advantage. Great entrepreneurs look lucky because they are quick to seize opportunities that come their way. They also know when to take a profit, as Dunstone did with his float and his deals with Best Buy and Dixons. By setting up Talk Talk, Dunstone also massively reduced the risk that Carphone could be cornered by the network providers who supplied his key source of turnover – an uncomfortable position that led to the downfall of Phones4U.

*

The corporately run chains that commissioned corporately designed shop fitting and made their product the star of the show should have known that their customers would need help from qualified sales assistants. Nearly everyone thinks they can run a shop, until they try for themselves: that's when they discover how hard it is to give great service.

Steve Jobs of Apple was so frustrated with the way retailers sold his products, he withdrew the franchise to sell Apple-Mac computers from a significant number of shops, and then decided to show them what to do by opening Apple's own stores.

Steve Jobs and the talented team he hired really went for it. They wanted to create the perfect shop for Apple users, so they put customer service on a new level. Customers were given tuition through hands-on experience. If anything could possibly be done to turn the Apple Store into the very best, that's what they did.

They look so good it is difficult to resist having a look inside. If you do you will not be alone; from the very first day Apple Stores were busy and the army of well-paid sales advisers have plenty to do. Steve Jobs realised that even the most confident-looking tech shopper may have difficulty working the latest gizmo. Hence the Genius Bar where help is on hand from an expert who won't ever make you feel a fool.

The experts said they couldn't possibly make money in a shop that cost so much to open, in a prime spot with lots of well-paid sales assistants who talked a lot about technology but didn't try to sell anything. The experts were wrong. The Apple Store beat everyone's forecast for customer traffic, turnover and profit. The concept is so different and so successful it has set a new gold standard for other retailers to follow. Apple Stores don't look like other shops and their customers often forget they are shopping, but between them they spend a lot of money.

Just at the time everyone was talking about online shopping via mobile and tablet causing lots of shops to close, along comes a brand new type of shop selling the very products predicted to end high street shopping. Twenty-five years ago there were no mobile phone shops but within ten years they were a significant part of the retail scene. The retail landscape has always been on the move, but as time goes by things change quicker and quicker.

It is well worth repeating that some of the biggest and most successful retailers 25 years from now have not yet set out in business and will be selling something that has not yet been invented.

GEOFF MULCAHY
AND THE DIY BUSINESS

You tend to think of entrepreneurs as self-made men or women who started their own business and built it into a big empire. Many of the people in this book fit that description, but a man who was at the middle of some of the biggest moves in retailing and certainly played a major part in reshaping the UK shopping scene was more of a professional manager and consultant than a shopkeeper.

Woolworths started in the USA. According to their company archives, in the late 1860s a young Frank Winfield Woolworth took a job as a shop assistant but when he failed to make the grade he was given the job of assembling the display of 5-cent goods. This was such a success that, with his employer's support, he eventually branched out with his own fixed-price store where the offer was extended to 10-cent items – and the rest is history. The American chain opened its first UK shop in Church Street, Liverpool in 1909, where the original 5c + 10c stores were translated into Threepenny and Sixpenny Stores, pretty much the pound store of the day. The sixpence price limit in Britain was retained until the Second World War.

I can vouch from personal experience that Woolworths stores were very busy. When I was about four I got separated from my mother and was lost among the crowd in the George Street store in Altrincham, where the old-fashioned counters and wooden floor resembled an indoor market. Woolworths was so successful, by 1958 they had 1,000 stores in the UK, but in the 1960s and 70s management failed to keep the low price formula fresh and fashionable.

The stores looked quaint and dated. On both sides of the Atlantic, Woolworths failed to find an up-to-date discount format and in 1982 when the parent company in the USA found itself short of cash, they sold their shares in the British company for £310m to a consortium of investors named Paternoster Stores masterminded by Victor Blank of Charterhouse Bank. It was one of the earliest and most imaginative venture capital deals in the UK.

Despite indecision by a conservative Woolworths management team who didn't know whether to start selling groceries and struggled to develop their out-of-town Woolco stores, they made one good move by buying B&Q, a developing DIY chain that had been started in 1969 near Southampton, by Richard Block and David Quayle (hence B&Q). The co-founders rapidly built the business to 26 stores before handing day to day control to the management team who made several acquisitions before selling to Woolworths.

Geoff Mulcahy was brought in by Paternoster Stores (which was soon renamed Woolworth Holdings) first as Finance Director before becoming chief executive. He came with a science degree from Manchester University, a Harvard MBA plus experience at Esso, British Sugar and Norton Abrasives (an American engineering company) and can best be described as a strategist. At British Sugar he worked with John Beckett who was at the centre of the Woolworths acquisition and approached Mulcahy to be the numbers man and help transform the ailing chain.

Mulcahy made up for his lack of retail knowledge by surrounding himself with an array of shopkeeping talent. Among the many graduates of the Mulcahy school of management are Archie Norman who went to Asda, Roger Holmes who went to Marks & Spencer, Stephen Robertson who ran The British Retail Consortium, Leo McKee now at BrightHouse, Angus Munroe who really made his name at Matalan and Jim Hodkinson who had a major influence on turning B&Q into a category killer, before controversy meant a move to run New Look.

When the Woolworths deal was first done commentators dubbed it 'Mission Impossible' but the Paternoster team had a very different perspective to previous Woolworths managers. Three simple moves put up profits and dramatically reduced the debt. Every Woolworths store was given a basic facelift with the merchandise rationalised into six categories: 1) home and garden, 2) toys, 3) stationery, 4) children's clothing, 5) fashion accessories, 6) sweets and entertainment. This focused range planning helped to clarify what Woolworths was about and created cash by reducing stock investment. An even bigger benefit to the bank balance came from a radical review of the property portfolio. Unprofitable shops were closed, including those in company-owned freeholds where the trading was too poor to afford the market rent. It was a good time to be selling retail property. With a number of chains, particularly the Burton Group, keen to expand, the freeholds were sold well beyond book value and most leases commanded a healthy premium. Increases in trading profit and a significant injection of cash that reduced borrowings quickly made the Paternoster deal look good, but the gem was B&Q. Geoff Mulcahy's big idea was to use the cash created from Woolworths to rapidly expand the B&Q estate. By the time Mulcahy took over as chairman the future of Woolworth Holdings mainly depended on his plans to grow B&Q. A measure of Mulcahy's success was the bid from Stanley Kalms's Dixons in 1986 which valued Woolworth Holdings at £1.75bn – over five times the price paid by Paternoster Stores less than four years earlier.

Mulcahy and his team changed the name of the group to Kingfisher which they intended to turn into a retail conglomerate with the emphasis on out-of-town retail parks. In 1984 they acquired Comet, the electrical chain, which in 1968 had been one of the earliest discount warehouse retailers, started by the Hollingbery family in Hull. By 1984 the business had over 200 outlets and agreed a sale to Harris Queensway (the carpet business developed by Philip Harris) for £152m, but the following day Harris was gazumped by Kingfisher's £177m knock out bid.

In 1987 they acquired Superdrug, the discount beauty and health chain founded by Ronald and Peter Goldstein in 1964. Superdrug was floated on the stock market in 1981 when there were over 300 shops and acquired by Kingfisher three years later. Mulcahy more than doubled the size of Superdrug, moving the business upmarket and opening out of town.

Mulcahy also took Kingfisher into Europe with the acquisition in 1993 of Darty, a French-based electrical chain and in 1998 a merger between B&Q and the French discount DIY retailer Castorama.

While Mulcahy was adding new companies under Kingfisher's conglomerate wing, the jewel in the crown continued to be B&Q which was a clear leader in the DIY market.

There were plenty of competitors but none matched the scale and expertise of B&Q.

Two of the weaker rivals were Do It All which was developed by W.H. Smith, and Payless which was originally a retail offshoot of Marley Tiles. Payless was one of the first to bring a modern DIY concept to the high street, replacing the traditional ironmongers.

Payless was bought by Ward White, a men's shoe manufacture whose chairman Philip Birch had transformed the company with the purchase of Halfords which he planned to grow in the newly emerging retail parks. At the end of the 80s Boots bought Ward White to diversify their retail portfolio.

Both Boots and W.H. Smith found DIY a difficult market so in 1990 they put Do it All and Payless together under the Do it All name. The merger did little to improve profits, W.H. Smith withdrew and Boots soon sold Do it All to Focus DIY, which also bought Wickes and Great Mills to become B&Q's biggest competitor in the UK. The other major player was Homebase, which was developed by Sainsbury's, usually on sites adjacent to their supermarkets. Homebase tripled in size with the probably unwise acquisition in 1995 of Texas Homecare from the Ladbroke Group. Sainsbury's sold the shops to venture capitalists Schroder Ventures in 2000, but gave B&Q a boost by selling them 28 prime development sites.

While all these mergers and acquisitions were going on B&Q just kept getting bigger and better. Home Depot in the USA provided Mulcahy with a simple example to follow, with their big stores stocking such a comprehensive range it put all their competitors in the shade. The bigger format B&Q Warehouses were particularly successful and the other UK

DIY retailers looked pale in comparison. For a time B&Q had a reputation for poor service – the employees concentrated on catching shoplifters rather than caring for customers. But a campaign to provide expert advice on home improvements and a drive to employ more elderly workers made a major difference to their customer service.

Mulcahy and his team had confounded the critics by turning a woeful Woolworths into a thriving retail group in the UK and in Europe. Superdrug was doubling in size, B&Q could do no wrong and even dear Woolies, despite still being desperately dull was producing a decent profit. But, like many other big company bosses, Mulcahy was constantly looking for the next big deal. He wanted Kingfisher to have a much bigger retail portfolio under its wing. In 1989 he cheekily turned the tables on Stanley Kalms and put in a £461m offer for the Dixon Group but the bid was blocked by the Monopolies and Mergers Commission.

Mulcahy was certainly ambitious. In 1999 he got into serious talks with Allan Leighton at Asda about a proposed merger that would create one of the top twenty retailers in the world, with only Walmart and Home Depot in a different league.

It seemed a marriage made in heaven and both Mulcahy and Leighton announced their enthusiasm for the deal. Kingfisher brought international expertise, the Ladybird brand from Woolworths, toiletries from Superdrug, electricals from Comet and the whole DIY world from B&Q. Asda was best placed of all the supermarkets to develop non-food, having made a major mark with their George clothing brand. Mulcahy was impressed with the big stores in the Asda chain and saw a cultural fit with so many of the Kingfisher alumni being part of the Asda team.

But one of the potentially biggest deals in UK retail history never happened. At the eleventh hour Asda chairman Archie Norman revealed he had accepted an approach from Walmart to acquire Asda for cash.

It was the turning point for Kingfisher and Geoff Mulcahy. Like a lot of his peers he was to find that when growth by acquisition comes to an end, breaking up the group is almost certain to follow.

Geoff Mulcahy did much better than most. Sears, Storehouse, and the Burton Group disintegrated. UDS was taken over by Hanson Trust which quietly split up and disappeared, but Kingfisher slimmed down and carried on.

Mulcahy stepped down from Kingfisher within three years of his Asda disappointment, but not before he had strengthened the Kingfisher DIY business by buying Screwfix and broken the ties with less successful parts of the group by selling Superdrug and floating off Woolworths with no freeholds and £200m of debt.

When he retired from Kingfisher in 2003 Mulcahy can have fairly claimed that he did a fantastic job for his shareholders. At the time of his retirement some commentators criticised Mulcahy for being an indecisive, shy man who lacked charisma. If those comments are justified, he achieved an amazing amount for someone with so many faults.

PRICE MERCHANTS

Price always plays a big part in retailing but most high street multiples in the second half of the twentieth century relied on a reputation for value rather than aiming to be the cheapest. Every sector had a cut-price leader – like Curtess Shoes, John Collier (which used to be called The Fifty Shilling Tailors) and Woolworths. When supermarkets became prominent, part of the appeal was price and certainly low price was the main attraction of the furniture, carpets and beds you could buy at retail parks. But the last fifteen years have seen a massive growth in low-price retailing, with the recession providing an ideal boost. The crisis in 2008 brought tough times to most shopkeepers but those who based their appeal on low prices received a big benefit.

Matalan is an early example of this new generation of low-price retailers. Market trader John Hargreaves had developed a chain of shops in the North-West of England called Jaymax, before spotting an idea while on holiday in the USA. Hargreaves opened his first Matalan Discount Club in Preston in 1985. His out-of-town store had the feeling of a cash and carry and customers who claimed a membership card could qualify for special discounts, but Matalan wasn't restricted to trade buyers; it was a cut-price store that relied on sourcing from the Far East or buying grey market branded goods to produce retail prices that undercut all their competitors. For a time Matalan looked like a category killer until other retailers caught up.

The Matalan package with free parking and massive discounts available to Matalan members was an amazing success. By using low-rent premises, buying at keen prices and keeping a close control on costs Hargreaves was able to build a big customer base at a healthy margin. In 1998 the company had grown to over 75 stores and was floated on the stock exchange at an overall value of more than £190m. It was destined to get much bigger with more than 200 shops making a profit of over £100m.

But Matalan soon found other retailers were keen to compete at the bottom end of the market, and their out-of-town warehouse approach was unlikely to attract the upmarket buyers who started to find it smart to spot great value fashion.

Tesco's F+F and George at Asda, which was helped by the experience of parent company Walmart, became serious competitors, but being attached to a supermarket made it difficult for these brands to attract the younger fashion customers. Few would want to go out clubbing in an outfit bought at Matalan, George, F+F or M&S.

I have never been a Matalan shopper but I became a great fan of Stermat, a chain of hardware stores in North Wales which has often come to my rescue, particularly in their branch in Valley on Anglesey. Their product range is so comprehensive I have used the store as part of a party game I call 'guess what you can't buy for your house and home from Stermat'. Despite nominating unlikely items like avocado dishes and a toasted sandwich maker, no one has chosen something that Stermat hasn't got in stock. The store is reminiscent of *The Two*

Ronnies' 'Four Candles' sketch. Fortunately for Timpson most ironmongers and hardware shops (who used to cut your keys) have disappeared, but one hardware store has developed into one of the big players in the cut-price shopping scene.

Wilkinsons started in 1930 when James Wilkinson opened his first shop in Leicester, a business (Wilkinson Hardware Stores) that his son Tony, who significantly got his early experience working at Woolworths, grew into a major multiple before he retired in 2005. It remained a family business run by cousins – Tony's niece Karin Swann and his daughter Lisa Wilkinson – until Karin left the board in 2014.

Despite providing an impressive range in an improbable mixture of merchandise from greenhouses to venetian blinds, I always found the business bland and boring until I visited their state-of-the-art warehouse near Worksop. Gordon Brown, their then chief executive who hosted my visit, proudly paraded the statistics. Wilkinsons' warehouse costs were well under half the Woolworths rate, helping to give customers the best prices. This was one of the reasons why Woolworths disappeared and Wilkinsons was one of those businesses that have flourished by offering a similar low-price strategy.

*

More competition came from TK Maxx, an offshoot of the American TJ Maxx. This was a discount warehouse with a younger appeal but the market was really shaken up by low-price high street chains like Primark, New Look and Peacocks.

Primark was launched when Arthur Ryan opened a store in Dublin branded Penneys using a £50,000 investment from Garfield Weston who was keen to develop a new chain of cut-price fashion stores. When Ryan started opening outside

Ireland he used a different name, 'Primark', to avoid any confusion with JCPenney. For some years Primark was a lacklustre business that made little impression on British buyers but all that changed when holding company Associated British Foods made a major dash for growth, first buying Littlewoods Stores for £409m, keeping 40 stores and selling on the rest, then purchasing a number of sites from the Woolworths and C&A portfolios. Suddenly Primark became a major fashion force, unexpectedly inspired by Arthur Price, whose staid and traditional training as a buyer for Swan & Edgar, followed by a spell at Dunnes Stores, had hardly prepared him to lead the team that produced a magic combination of pretty high fashion at rock bottom prices.

By selling big volumes and buying from the Far East at an unbelievably low cost, Primark provided teenagers with the chance to fill their wardrobe simply by spending their pocket money. I was amazed one Saturday night when Beth, an ex-foster child who recently came back to live with us, came home with three big bags of skirts, tops, trousers, shoes, socks, hats and shoes (not just one outfit, several). She claimed the whole lot had cost her less than £100. I didn't believe her until I saw the receipt for £96.28. No wonder Primark has done so well and created such shock waves along every high street and shopping mall.

*

Wilkinsons (now known as Wilko) was a hardware store that expanded its range, but the latest cut-price shops set out without any particular product base; their unique selling proposition was to be as cheap as possible. The principle was established in the UK at the beginning of the 20th century by Woolworths when the concept of their Five and Ten Cent Stores crossed the Atlantic and their first Threepenny and Sixpenny Store opened in Liverpool in 1909. As every retailer knows, customers will buy anything if it is cheap enough, especially if they are allowed to rummage in a bargain bin. Today's pound shops have taken major retail spaces and turned them into big bargain basements.

It might still be more fashionable to become an internet retailer but some of the most successful shopkeepers since 1990 have developed low-price pound shops on the Jack Cohen principle of piling it high and selling it cheap, but instead of 3d and 6d the magic price is now £1.

It isn't surprising that our traditional covered markets have had a rough time. The £1 stores have taken market trading on to the traditional high street. To be successful these discount shops have to keep costs down – totally self-service, low rent per square foot with an ultra-efficient distribution and warehouse system – but the real key is a keen team of buyers who can spot opportunistic deals. They do not need to provide a balanced range of merchandise or have the same range month in month out, but they must always offer fantastic value. Hence the need for opportunistic buying. Bankrupt stock, over production and grey supplies of well-known brands at a big discount give discount stores the chance to keep their promise of amazing value.

Home Bargains, founded in Liverpool by Tom Morris who started retailing in 1976 and launched the Home Bargains brand in the 1980s, is the longest established of the modern cut-price retailers. Home Bargains remains an independent family business, but boosted by the acquisition of several old Kwik Save and Woolworths stores has grown to over 300 stores.

*

Another 300-plus chain, Poundstretcher, is almost as long established as Home Bargains, having started in Huddersfield in 1983, but has not had such a trouble-free path to success. The founders sold out to Brown and Jackson which not only changed the name of their group to '...instore' but decided to convert half the Poundstretcher fascia to '...instore' in an unwise attempt to move upmarket. All the fascias were moving back to Poundstretcher when the shops were acquired in 2009 by Rashid and Aziz Tayub who came to the UK from Malawi and now have 400 Poundstretcher shops with an uncompromising cut-price formula.

The Poundstretcher story shows that cut-price retail success isn't that simple, but anyone would think so if they just looked at the meteoric growth Simon and Bobby Arora achieved after buying 21 B&M stores in 2004, a business which was valued at £2.7bn when the 400 store business was floated in 2014.

The Arora family not only found a fantastic retail format, they worked out how to achieve rapid growth without breaking the bank. Under their guidance B&M took the chance to acquire sites from the wreckage of Woolworths, Kwik Save and Focus DIY. With a rapid stock turn and extended payment terms they were often able to sell their merchandise before it was paid for. As they opened more shops and increased sales, more cash came into the B&M coffers.

The Arora family are still very much involved in the management, even after receiving one big payout when they sold a significant tranche of stores to venture capitalists in 2012 and a second big pay day in 2014, but you wonder how long it will be before the pressures of City analysts and institutions put process-driven management into a company built on flair and instinct.

*

By definition 99p Stores is the cheapest in the cut-price sector, if only by a penny. Unlike many of its competitors, 99p Stores was launched in London when Nadir Lalani opened his first shop in Holloway in 2001.

Lalani came to the UK from Tanzania in 1971 and during the next fourteen years built up a chain of fifteen convenience stores which he sold to Naresh and Mahesh Patel who renamed the shops Europa Foods and, after adding the Cullens Convenience stores, sold the business to Tesco for £53.7 million when the stores were rebranded 'Tesco Express'.

Lalani planned to concentrate on property, but soon decided that he was better suited to shopkeeping. In 1991 he bought two convenience stores, branded Whistlestop, in railway stations, a business he expanded to 27 outlets before deciding to sell up, enter the discount business, and open his first 99p Stores outlet. His plan was to find a buyer and retire by 2008, but it took him much longer for 99p Stores to match the profitability of his Northern-based competitors. Eventually, in 2015 he agreed a sale, when Poundland offered £55m for 251 stores, only to find the deal was delayed by the Competition and Markets Authority on competitive grounds.

*

Poundland should not be confused with Poundworld, which was founded by father and son Chris Edwards junior and senior, who set up a market stall in Wakefield in 1974. In 1997 the

Edwards' business switched to a single-price strategy under the fascia 'Everything's £1' which was changed in 2004 to Poundworld and while still being firmly under family control started rapidly expanding to a chain of over 280 stores with a turnover of more than £300m by May 2015, when the family sold the business to US private equity firm TPG for £150m.

Back to Poundland which, like B&M, have floated on the stock exchange and can be expected to seek more acquisitions to satisfy the growth ambitions of their institutional shareholders.

Poundland started in 1990 as a single store in the Octagon Centre, Burton on Trent, opened by market traders Steve Smith and David Dodd, who claimed that Poundland was the first genuine, single-price, pound shop. Like other successful discount shop pioneers they took cut-price retailing out of the usual world of secondary sites and run-down fittings and put it into the mainstream shopping centres. David Dodd retained a 12 per cent stake when the business was bought out by venture capitalists Advent International in 2002, by which time there were 75 shops. This had risen to 150 stores in 2006 when Jim McCarthy joined as chief executive after senior management experience with Dillons, T&S Stores and Sainsbury's Local.

McCarthy was faithful to the single-price format which allowed the business to prosper by selling an unlikely product range – a motley collection of merchandise including spanners and sandwiches, hair grips and shampoo. You could never be certain what McCarthy would be selling at Poundland but you could guarantee that the price would be £1.

In 2010 Poundland, with sales now approaching £400m from 260 shops, changed hands again, when Advent sold to rival buyout company Warburg Pincus. McCarthy was able to cash in his management shares and invest in the re-geared business which he continued to run as chief executive. By then discount shops were no longer regarded as downmarket bazaars that had no place on a proper high street. In a property world hit by recession and facing falling rents and empty shops, discount retailers were suddenly made to feel warmly welcome. In 2010 lots of big shops were going into administration and landlords had loads of sites they needed to fill. It was the perfect time to be a growth business and Jim McCarthy took full advantage.

In 2014, with nearly 500 shops, Poundland was floated on the stock market at a market value of £750m, and it took only a matter of months to use its new financial strength to make an offer for 99p Stores and potentially create a group with nearly 800 discount shops.

*

Since 2008, £1 stores and discount shops have almost all been getting bigger and doing better. When Woolworths disappeared, a new generation of entrepreneurs more than filled the gap they left on the high street. But the new boys' current success story may not continue for ever. Those companies that now have institutional shareholders will want to grow and may tempt the remaining entrepreneur owners to achieve their exit and buy a ski chalet, a home in the Caribbean and the plane to travel between the two.

Cut-price retailing is not as simple as it seems, especially if you are in the fashion business. There are plenty of examples of companies with very keen prices that failed to turn amazing value into sales and profit success.

Ethel Austin, a cheap and cheerful Liverpool-based fashion

chain founded in 1934, grew to 300 stores, mainly in North Wales and the North-West of England. But when other budget price chains found that the recession boosted business, Ethel Austin entered administration in 2008. Over the next four years the company set some sort of record by going into administration three more times, in 2010, 2012 and finally in 2013. This record shows that even the cheapest shops need the right products in great stores. It is difficult to revive an ailing retailer.

The Scottish retailer Mackays, which now trades as M&Co, has been more successful. I got to know their shops in the 1980s when I opened shoe concessions in the most unlikely set of locations, Sittingbourne in Kent as well as Cramlington and Seaham, both in the North-East of England. In those days Mackays were half-way between an old-fashioned department store and a cut-price clothes shop. It suited the Timpson shoe shop customers but with the stores being controlled by Scottish prudence it was retailing on a shoe string.

The move from Mackays to M&Co has helped the company keep a 260-shop stake in the budget retail business.

Peacocks looked like a cut-price success story until an over-geared management buyout in 2005 came back to bite them. Peacock's Penny Bazaar started in Warrington in the 1880s and eventually, in the 1940s moved their headquarters to Cardiff and expanded into the South of England. It remained a family business until going public in 1999. Six years later chief executive Richard Kirk led a hedge-fund-backed management buyout. Before the buyout Peacocks had about £70m of net debt which soared as a result of the deal to £460m. Keen to create growth and a valuable exit, the privatised Peacocks invested in an aggressive expansion programme, fitting out new shops in high rented sites. Debts rose to £700m and the poor shop managers were only just producing enough profit to pay the interest. The recession didn't come to the rescue and with better competitors down the street Peacocks went into administration leaving a lot of empty spaces in some of our biggest shopping centres.

*

Even one of the most successful value fashion retailers has had a bit of a roller coaster ride. Founder Tom Singh, who started the business in Weymouth, developed New Look into the most successful budget price fast fashion store until Primark claimed such a commanding position in the market.

Tom Singh created an excellent business with real value for young fashion customers including the best own-brand shoe department in any clothing shop.

The business had some ups and downs, partly due to the recession but mainly through brilliant buying one season and a few missed fashion trends a year later. Company performance wasn't helped by changes of ownership. A float was followed by a venture-capital-backed buyout and another proposed float that never happened. While all this was going on Tom Singh was in and out of control.

The company, founded in 1969, was floated on the stock exchange in 1998 but in 2004 a £1.2m deal took the company private with Tom Singh retaining a 25 per cent stake. Plans to refloat the company in 2010 never came to fruition and with the company encountering a rough period of trading Tom Singh rekindled his executive interest in New Look.

Perhaps New Look is another example that shows the instinctive flair of a founding entrepreneur is more than a match for the processes produced by professional managers.

Singh was able to sell the business in May 2015 for £780m to South African investment company Brait SA.

*

No chapter about cut-price retail would be complete without mentioning Aldi and Lidl, who could be called the Ryanair of retailing, businesses that use a no frills approach to keep prices as low as possible and undercut all their competitors.

When Aldi and Lidl, both based in Germany, came to the UK most shoppers viewed them with contempt, to be used only if you couldn't afford anything else. Few people wanted to be labelled as an Aldi or Lidl shopper.

Since 2010 that perception has changed. With the help of the media, which have consistently poured praise on these German invaders as they grabbed market share from the main supermarkets, Aldi and Lidl have become the smart place to shop.

This new format caught out the complacent super-markets who were still building bigger stores with a wider product selection when their customers were happy with the smaller selection in Aldi and Lidl that made shopping less complicated.

Supermarkets are now fully aware of the new threat and we can expect them to follow suit by producing their own version of limited choice with amazing value. Some commentators and market analysts have suggested that Aldi and Lidl have been boosted by a change of routine to more frequent purchases in preference to the big weekly or fortnightly shop. I am not so sure; my regular visits to Tesco and Sainsbury's suggest that the same number of customers still come to the checkouts, but perhaps the trolleys aren't quite as full.

Aldi and Lidl have played an important part in a major shift in UK retailing that, among other things, has shown that the massive Tesco now needs to get better rather than bigger. In 2014, despite there being no growth in the grocery sector, Aldi increased sales by 22 per cent and Lidl by 15 per cent. The question to ask now is how much more can these businesses grow before they too get too big?

Cut-price retail has produced some of the most successful new retailers of the last decade, but the next generation of budding entrepreneurs will almost certainly need to completely update the format to avoid following in Woolworths' footsteps.

COMEBACK KIDS

I will never forget the merchant banker who told me: 'I'm an expert at putting professional management into family businesses.' Over the next four years he provided dramatic proof that he had got it totally wrong. He'd just bought Mister Minit, a global shoe repair chain that had been owned by Don Hilsdon Ryan, an American based in Switzerland who built Mister Minit from a single concession opened in a Brussels department store in 1957. I wanted to buy the British bit, but got a blunt refusal with the comment: 'You are next on my list!'

It worked the other way round: the bank (UBS) lost £120m in the UK during the next four years and we were able to buy the shops we wanted for £1.

I mention a number of businesses in this book that finished in administration. Most would never have existed if it hadn't been for a creative entrepreneur who worked hard to build up the business by following his instinct. Few started out with a business plan, most pursued an idea and while turning it into an enterprise learnt about management along the way.

The merchant banker may have had, at the back of his mind, 'clogs to clogs in three generations' and in many companies that is what happens, but the third generation is often someone from outside the family. Professional management can be a poor substitute for the flair of a pioneer.

It is foolish to generalise. Of course there are companies like Next and John Lewis that have taken management changes in their stride but others such as M&S and Morrisons struggle to make them work.

I believe good management has more to do with ideas and people than business plans and process and I think this theory is reinforced by the number of entrepreneurs who have made a success out of the same business for a second time.

*

The classic example of a comeback kid is Malcolm Walker of Iceland, whose autobiography *Best Served Cold* must be just about the best business book to take on holiday – an easy-to-read yarn with plenty of twists, turns and outrageous comments along the way.

Malcolm created controversy from the start by setting up his first business while he still had a full-time job with Woolworths. He got the sack, which in retrospect was just what he needed to turn his first shop in Oswestry (not the liveliest place to start) into a success. Thirteen years later he floated Iceland with a stock market offer that was 113 times oversubscribed. It was a great business with a simple formula that got even better and bigger when Malcolm won a battle to buy southern-based freezer chain Bejam, creating a national chain of 465 shops which competed with the fast-growing supermarket chains by developing a wide range of new products and being the first food retail chain to offer free home delivery. But in the late 90s Malcolm made life complicated by taking on £600m of debt to buy Booker, the UK's leading cash and carry business. The principles that applied to Iceland were not going to provide answers at Booker but Malcolm wasn't too bothered; the experienced Stuart Rose had taken over the role of Group chief executive and Malcolm stepped up to chairman as a logical move towards retirement.

But you never know what will happen next. Stuart Rose left in 2001 to take the vacant job at Arcadia and Malcolm made a major error by appointing Bill Grimsey, who previously had managed Wickes DIY, as Group chief executive. The company changed overnight. Instead of having a team who were focused on helping branch colleagues to increase sales and enjoy their job, the new head office spent their time buried in meetings and office politics. Within weeks of joining Iceland Bill Grimsey, together with financial director Bill Hoskins who also came from Wickes, identified massive problems, listed £145m of exceptional costs and declared a loss for the year of £120m.

Meanwhile, Malcolm, as part of his retirement plan, sold £13.5m of Iceland shares without realising that within weeks the company would be forced to issue a profit warning. When Tesco's supplier problems led to a profit warning in 2014 we saw how quickly a company's reputation can be undermined. The same happened to Iceland – within weeks the company had changed from an investor's favourite into a share to avoid.

Malcolm left, with the prospect of an investigation into insider or fraudulent dealing, which was dropped three years later. Although he talked of a life of leisure in the Maldives, Malcolm quickly got back to business by starting a new frozen food chain, called Cooltrader, around Merseyside.

For four years Bill Grimsey failed to find a formula to

revive the fortunes of Iceland, which he renamed The Big Food Group. Despite a succession of recovery plans, sales steadily declined and Bill Grimsey ended his misery in 2005 by accepting a bid from Baugur, the Icelandic investment group that was just starting a rapid and reckless acquisition programme, picking up a selection of poor-performing retailers.

The Baugur deal split The Big Food Group back into its component parts with Booker becoming a separate company and Malcolm Walker getting management control and a minority shareholding of Iceland.

Malcolm brought in several members of his old team and went back to the formula that created his original success. It was his instinct for what works that made Iceland into a big business and nothing had changed. He always concentrates on giving customers what they want and looking after the colleagues who help him run his shops. He was the first to see the appeal of round pound pricing.

Malcolm knew how to reverse the Grimsey errors and put a common sense approach back into the shops. But he provided an extra bit of magic: simply by coming back he put a big smile on the faces of those who had been working for him four years earlier. Malcolm is an inspirational leader who colleagues trust. Under Bill Grimsey Iceland lost its culture, Malcolm brought it back.

The result was stunning. The chain that The Big Food Group was struggling to turn into profit suddenly took off, with sales rising more than 10 per cent a year for four years running and gross profits climbing to nearly £200m.

It got even better for Malcolm in 2012. Helped by co-investors that included Lord Kirkham, Malcolm bought out the Baugur shareholding and became chairman and chief executive. With his management team he controls 43 per cent of the equity in a business valued at £1.45 billion.

Not a bad deal for a guy who started the company with an investment of £30 into a shop in Oswestry. But it isn't just the money, it is difficult to put a price on the satisfaction Malcolm must have got from coming back in from the cold to show how it should be done.

*

Philip Harris was born into the carpet business. As a teenager he inherited three carpet shops when his father died and, initially helped by his mother, expanded the business. First he added one shop at a time but big expansion came in 1977 when he bought Queensway Carpets and a year later floated the company.

Harris, with his group now known as Harris Queensway, went on a spending spree buying a collection of other retailers including Times Furnishing, General George, Carpetland, and somewhat strangely, Hamley's the toy retailer. This last acquisition came from the rationalisation of Debenhams after their acquisition by Burton. My company, Timpson, is another that could have joined the Harris collection. Philip Harris worked closely with Gerald Ronson, who early in 1983 launched a bid for United Drapery Stores of which Timpson was then a part. In return for supporting the bid, Ronson offered Harris first refusal on the shoe companies – Timpson and John Farmer.

The diversification wasn't helped by a drop in retail demand in the late 80s. Harris seemed more comfortable selling carpets than furniture or toys. There was a slump in profits but Harris found the answer by doing a deal with James Gulliver who led a management buy-in. Harris sold his shares but never signed a 'no-competition clause'. Within two years the newly named Lowndes Queensway buy-in went bust, but by then Harris was busy building another carpet chain, Carpetright, starting with one shop in Canning Town and quickly expanding with the purchase of Carpetland (a company that had been bought by Lowndes Queensway management), and the acquisition of Allied Carpets from Asda who were looking to concentrate on their supermarkets.

Despite a difficult start during tough times on the high street, Harris did well. He made more money by concentrating on carpets, a world he knew, loved and thoroughly understood. By 1996 Philip Harris was able to float his second carpet company and make another personal fortune.

One of his employees described Harris as 'probably the best carpet merchant in the world'. Most of us would be baffled by the tricky world of carpet shops with all their stock and special offers but Harris loved it. Few people would ever be able to make even a modest amount of money out of carpets, never mind a fortune. Philip Harris has done it twice.

*

Tom Farmer started a tyre retailing company when he was 23 and before he reached 30 sold it for £450,000 and retired to the USA, but he returned to Edinburgh two years later in 1971 to do it all over again under the name Kwik Fit.

As a franchise business Farmer was able to grow Kwik Fit quickly both in the UK and Europe. The idea of a multiple chain of car mechanics sounds simple but no one has done it better than Tom Farmer with his high standards of training, good housekeeping, and distinctive outlets that created a reputation for good service backed with the slogan 'You can't get better than a Kwik Fit fitter'.

For 28 years Farmer grew his business, helped by the constantly increasing number of motorists and the requirement for regular MOT testing. In 1999 Tom Farmer sold Kwik Fit to the Ford Motor Company for £1.2 billion, a fair price for a market leader with a brand that could be developed in other ways connected to the motoring world, like insurance. Ford only kept the business for three years before selling it to venture capitalists CVC, who in turn sold it on, in 2005, to another investment house, PAI Partners, for £800m, suggesting that Tom Farmer sold out at the top of the market. But perhaps professional managers found it difficult to follow in his footsteps. Although a chain of car repair workshops doesn't sound difficult to run, there are bound to be tricks of the trade that Tom Farmer learnt along the way. These are no doubt still put into practice in Farmer Autocare, based in Tom Farmer's native Scotland and his third start-up in the same market, which shows how entrepreneurs never lose the golden touch that for some can bring success many times over.

*

My final comeback kid is Graham Kirkham, developer of DFS, the furniture chain. Graham didn't disappear like my previous examples but he still managed to make two fortunes out of the same business.

Like all these serial entrepreneurs Graham wasn't a business graduate and didn't even, like many in this book, inherit the seed corn of a business from his parents. Having left school at sixteen he started work as a salesman in a furniture shop. At the age of 24 he had his own business making furniture above a shop, where he sold the finished product, in Carcroft near Doncaster in Yorkshire.

It worked. By both making and selling sofas, chairs and tables he was able to cut out the middle man and make real money. Five years later he opened a second shop, then his big break came when he bought one of his biggest suppliers, Direct Furnishing Supplies (DFS), out of bankruptcy, bringing him a chain of 63 shops.

To me the idea of selling furniture with its high stock turn and fickle demand is a nightmare but Graham Kirkham was totally at ease – he instinctively knew how to motivate his team and bring in the customers. He understood the importance of giving good value and setting deadlines. The 'never to be repeated' price offer that 'must end on Saturday' was the best way to bring in the customers, and he spent over £1 billion on advertising to prove it. But, when customers arrived at a DFS store, he made sure there was plenty of stock available and keen sales assistants who gave the right combination of hard sell and helpful customer service along with loads of free credit. Graham made a point of visiting his stores and his personality came across in the way they did business.

In 1993 DFS was floated at a market value of £271m but remained as a public company for less than ten years before Graham Kirkham took the chain private again in a leveraged buyout that valued the business at nearly £500m. A substantial part of the Kirkham shareholding was sold in 2012 when the company was acquired by another private equity firm, Advent.

*

My comeback kids have made two or even three fortunes out of the same business, and demonstrated how much the founder knows about his company. It was foolish for the banker to suggest he could put professional managers into a family business and produce an instant improvement. Companies are rarely created by luck. The founding family will have detailed know-how that isn't taught at business school. As my comeback heroes show, that knowledge can be worth a fortune or even two.

MAIL ORDER

As I revealed in the introduction to the book, this journey through the world of retailing does not include a diversion online, so Jeff Bezos of Amazon, Martha Lane-Fox who helped create lastminute.com and John Roberts of AO.com are not included in my list of greatest retailers. I haven't, however, excluded their home shopping predecessors.

When I was buying shoes for our shoe shops I became acutely aware of the competition from mail order. In the value footwear business, catalogue shopping claimed about 10 per cent of the market. With a well-established network of agents, several copies of the main catalogues such as Littlewoods, Grattan, Kays and Freemans were scattered around our office, where many of our colleagues were attracted by convenience and credit to pay a pretty full price for a wide range of products from fashion to garden furniture. Credit has always been an important part of shopping but the interest rates charged in the 1960s by multiple tailors using hire purchase and door-to-door salesmen pushing Provident cheques never felt as pernicious as the present cost of buying on tick from BrightHouse or taking out a pay day loan.

The Fattorini family had a significant influence on the development of mail order in the UK. Antonio Fattorini, who came to Britain from Italy in 1815, using his retail jewellery business as a base, created Fattorini Watch Clubs. Groups of customers, often in pubs, would form a club which required a regular weekly subscription of a few pence. In total it was enough to buy a watch each week. The members drew lots to decide the order in which the watches were distributed.

Antonio had seven sons who developed the business into mail order, which in 1910 was named Empire Stores. Two years later Enrico Fattorini fell out with his brothers and started his own business, Grattan Warehouses.

Another jeweller who moved into mail order was Kilbourne Kay, who produced a catalogue to support his shop in Worcester in 1890. At first the catalogue was full of jewellery, watches and household items but in the 1900s clothing was included and the Kay's catalogue started to grow into a significant business.

Littlewoods was created by John Moores, who had already made a fortune of over £1m from Littlewoods football pools, which he started in 1923. In a similar way to the Fattorinis, John Moores created shilling clubs by recruiting customers who were already on his football pool mailing list.

The first Littlewoods catalogue, of 166 pages, was published in May 1932. By 1936 Moores, a man blessed with a magic touch, had another success on his hands, the catalogue hit £4m turnover and Moores was a mail order millionaire. A year later he spotted a third Littlewoods opportunity and opened his first store in Blackpool. By the beginning of the Second World War he had a chain of 24 stores.

Freemans mail order catalogue was named after one of its four founding partners. Based in London, the catalogue, established in 1905 and specialising in clothing, was distributed throughout the UK and in the 1930s the company claimed to be the country's biggest mail order operation with over 30,000 agents. The company was floated on the stock exchange in 1963 and, with sales still increasing, an enormous automated warehouse was opened in Peterborough in 1969. I visited this warehouse several years later and was amazed by its awesome size and calm efficiency.

In 1988 Freemans was acquired by Sears, just before this giant retail conglomerate went into free fall, so Freemans finished in the hands of Philip Green who quickly found a buyer, the German mail order company Otto Versand.

Universal Stores (Manchester) Ltd was started in 1900 as a mail order business by brothers Abraham, George and Jack Rose. The business did well and in 1931, after the name had been changed to Great Universal Stores, the company was floated on the London Stock Exchange. Business suffered as a result of the Great Depression and the now public company made a loss.

With perfect timing Isaac Wolfson, a salesman who impressed George Rose at a trade exhibition, arrived to take on the role of GUS's merchandise controller. Within two years he was running the business and the company quickly recovered.

Isaac Wolfson was one of the few people alongside Charles Clore to recognise the significance of undervalued property on a retailer's balance sheet. It often meant that he could acquire a company by paying considerably more than the book value but fund the purchase by selling a proportion of the property portfolio.

Wolfson's most significant deal was the purchase of the Kay catalogue company in 1943, but he expanded Great Universal Stores way beyond mail order. His retail subsidiaries included Times Furnishing, Greenlees and Easiephit footwear,

Paige (ladies' wear), Waring & Gillow and Burberry. Isaac Wolfson always had his eye on Timpson and contacted my father almost every year to see whether we would sell him our business.

His attempt to acquire Empire Stores was blocked by the Monopolies and Mergers Commission but in 1981 he was able to pick up John Myers Home Shopping from the UDS Group, a deal I observed from the other side because Timpson, another UDS subsidiary at that time, was based only ten miles from the John Myers head office in Stockport. I saw enough during our futile attempts to help John Myers after their shock announcement of a £23m loss to realise that Isaac Wolfson must have been paid money to take John Myers off their hands.

After Isaac's son Leonard was handed control he recognised that many of their retail companies had tired trading formats so he sold over 2,000 shops but still retained their property assets, while mail order remained the main part of GUS.

When Leonard's cousin David took over as chief executive the company had a reputation for having a lot of cash and few ideas. David soon changed that by purchasing Experian, a first big step towards building a financial and business services division. This seemed to signal a move away from mail order but his next acquisition, Argos, was a bold move to expand into another part of the catalogue business. This was followed by the purchase of Index, the Littlewoods' catalogue shops.

In 2003 the catalogue business was sold to the Barclay brothers, the publicity-shy twins based in the Channel Islands.

The main UK mail order businesses are now in two groups. Otto Versand, the world's largest mail order company based in Germany, owns Freemans and Grattan, while the Barclay brothers have Littlewoods, Great Universal, Kay, Empire Stores and Marshall Ward.

One mail order company has, however, remained fiercely independent.

JD Williams was a family business for over a century before it was acquired by David Alliance who put it into his property company, N Brown Group plc. While pursuing a hyperactive career creating one of the world's biggest textile groups employing 70,000 people in 67 countries, David Alliance found time to turn N Brown into a highly successful mail order company with a collection of specialist brands, particularly catering for mature customers and those seeking less popular sizes. (I remember the difficulty of supplying shoes in size 2 for women and size 13 for men through a chain of retail shops; it is so much easier to sell through a catalogue which is supplied by one warehouse.)

David Alliance, who remained chairman until 2012 and is still a non-executive director, kept N Brown focused on niche markets where mail order works really well and encouraged the company to evolve into a multi-channel retailer with a strong presence in e-commerce.

With Next and John Lewis developing a substantial and presumably profitable online business combined with the option to Click and Collect, there seems little doubt that online sales will become a big part of retail. In the meantime I am happy to reflect on the retail heroes who made their money out of mail order. E-commerce superstars will have to wait before they qualify for my hall of fame.

ANITA RODDICK

If Anita Roddick had presented her original business idea on *Dragons' Den* she would have been rejected with a few caustic comments from the panel. No one would have offered to invest in a shop based in Brighton selling sixteen lines of quirky cosmetics in refillable bottles run by a woman with no business experience, who was simply hoping to make some money while her husband was away travelling.

I first heard about The Body Shop when the business only had two shops. I was involved in a TV programme for the Open University (the broadcast was repeated several times but always in the middle of the night). Half the programme featured the Timpson Code of Customer Service, the other half was about this wacky woman who was selling eco-friendly cosmetics. Anita Roddick might have started without any management expertise but she soon worked out how to attract publicity.

Anita Roddick was a rebel with a cause. It isn't clear whether The Body Shop was inspired by her frugal mother's hatred of waste, her world travels that took her face-to-face with tribal customs and native body treatments, or a visit to an earlier version of Body Shop in California. Whatever the inspiration it was hardly a good preparation for running a business. With no experience, no planning and no training, The Body Shop just happened. It was an accident that worked.

The timing was perfect. The world was going green and it was suddenly fashionable to have a social conscience. People cared about waste, recycling, protecting the environment and fair trading. The Body Shop wasn't just selling cosmetics – it also offered 'correct' political values. With its distinctive logo, innovative products and green fascia, the whole concept provided a perfect package for franchising, with a special appeal to potential franchisees who were attracted by becoming part of an environmentally friendly business. To cap it all, retailing was heading for the age of niche business, when sharply focused small shops were a favourite with the City. The Body Shop float was a stunning stock market success alongside Tie Rack and Sock Shop.

Despite the benefit of perfect timing, you can't put the success of The Body Shop down to pure luck. Anita Roddick must have been a great organiser with the ability to pick some good people to join her team. It isn't easy to develop a chain of shops from scratch. There are some key crunch points to overcome. Opening the second shop means you have to trust someone to look after a store – you can't be in two places at once. To go beyond fifteen shops you need to appoint an area manager; once you get to 30 branches even the most hands-on chief executive will take more than a month to visit every shop. Franchising helped find the finance for Body Shop to grow quickly but none of this would have been possible without a range of management skills including merchandising, property and distribution.

Body Shop had a very strong culture which covered every aspect of the shop from the green fascia to the campaigning posters, but customers needed to know they were buying the real thing – all the stock must have natural ingredients bought from fair trade sources. Anita Roddick was on a mission to find merchandise that made a real difference to manufacturers in poor parts of the world. Hence the Footsie Roller that was made in Southern India and, nearer to home, the Soapworks factory Anita Roddick set up in Easterhouse, then a high unemployment district of Glasgow. But the mission went beyond the stock held on the shelves. The big aim was 'To dedicate our business to the pursuit of social and environmental change'. The stores were used as a soapbox to promote a crusade and the message on the hard-hitting posters meant so much more because they were created by the boss. It is much easier for the company's owner to set a culture that others will follow. The presence of Victor Kiam, Richard Branson and Bernard Matthews put extra power into their own advertising. Anita Roddick put all her personality into The Body Shop.

The company's eco-friendly credentials made it attractive to franchisees, employees and customers who saw ethical consumption as a way of voting for the good guys.

The Body Shop float in 1988 was a fantastic success but the Roddicks were never so sure, suggesting Body Shop lost its soul when it became a quoted company. They learnt the simple lesson that you need 100 per cent of the equity to do exactly what you want. They made two or three attempts to get the business back, but by then they had been so successful the company was too expensive to be bought back without the help of bank support. Once floated, the Body Shop campaign had to keep within the City investors' limits.

Despite the Roddicks' scepticism The Body Shop still stuck to its campaigning culture as a public company. Shareholders clearly saw that to continue to produce profit growth, the shops needed to stay on the moral high ground. Anita Roddick may not have been able to get every shop to back her pet campaign to publicly criticise the World Trade Organization, but there was never any doubt where Body Shop and the Roddicks stood on fair trade and the environment.

Anita Roddick did a lot for another cause that was beyond her brief. She helped to raise the status of women in business and inspire other women to follow in her footsteps. The current campaigners for more women in the boardroom probably don't appreciate how much of the glass ceiling was broken when Body Shop floated in 1988.

People who campaign for causes with conviction often get even more passionate and ambitious as they grow older. When Anita Roddick stepped back from day-to-day management, a greater percentage of her life was devoted to the original promise 'To dedicate our business to the pursuit of social and environmental change'.

By the time Body Shop became part of L'Oréal in 2006 the business was operating in 60 markets around the world and had nearly 2,500 stores – an amazing development from the single shop in Brighton run by someone with no experience of business.

Anita Roddick didn't see her job as having much to do with finance and quality management. To her, being an entrepreneur meant you needed a mission with principles and ideas. She admired the Quaker firms that put people first and didn't see why every company couldn't be run the same way. Many of us learnt a lot of lessons from the way she built Body Shop.

WOMEN IN RETAIL

Anita Roddick was a great role model for women in retailing, showing how to enter what, for most of the 20th century, was a man's world and come out on top.

Retailing has given many more jobs to women than men, but when I started my career in the 1960s very few women got anywhere near the boardroom. At the Timpson office in Wythenshawe, I walked into a workplace where status was very important. Executives had allocated parking bays, each with a number. The lower the number, the higher you were on the company pecking order. There were four levels of dining room – directors', senior executives', junior executives' and the canteen. We also had executive lavatories but there was no need for a posh ladies' loo because the most senior women were Miss Creasey who ran the typing pool and Doris Ferguson our welfare officer (after a bit of a battle they were allowed to use the junior executives' dining room).

We hadn't moved on much by 1973, when I was asked to run the 60-shop Swears & Wells chain. We employed 400 people, of whom only four of us were men – one managed the branch in Belfast, another was the van driver and two of us were directors.

Things are different today in Max Spielmann, our photo business – eleven out of our twelve area managers are women and they report to Sue who runs the business. So if anyone is concerned that my top 50 list at the end of this book has very few women included, I would like to make it clear that I am commenting on a period when that was just the way it was. A list drawn up in 2050 may well have more women than men.

More recently several retailers have promoted women into the top job. Belinda Earl, after early experience at Harrods, worked her way up the Debenhams management team from menswear merchandiser to chief executive in 1991, a position she later held at Jaeger before becoming style director at M&S.

Jill McDonald, after seven successful years running McDonald's in the UK and Northern Europe, in 2015 secured the chief executive job at Halfords.

Melissa Potter, who became chief executive of Clarks Shoes in 2010, joined the company straight from university and started her career on the company graduates' course. (I was an undistinguished participant on the same course 30 years earlier!)

Clarks, once the UK's top shoe manufacturer, has closed all its factories and the brand is now entirely made overseas, but since the collapse of British Shoe Corporation Clarks have been the leading UK shoe retailer, a position Melissa has consolidated while building a massive wholesale and retail business around the world.

The biggest retailer now in female hands is B&Q where Véronique Laury was promoted from Castorama to succeed Ian Cheshire as chief executive, following his retirement. But the biggest shake up must have been achieved by Kate Swann who was CEO of W.H. Smith for ten years until she left to run the food and beverage business SSP Group, which operates retail and catering outlets in 29 countries, specialising in airports and railway stations.

Before joining W.H. Smith, Kate Swann was Managing Director of Homebase and Argos. When she arrived at W.H. Smith the company was losing £135m a year and the chain of high street shops seemed doomed. Ten years later it was making profits of over £100m. She achieved this turnaround by ruthlessly sticking to some basic principles. On the high street, poor margin and low-growth products were thrown out, particularly music and DVDs, while at the same time staff levels were cut and expenditure was tightly controlled. Any investment was put into W.H. Smith Travel, the prosperous part of the group.

Kate Swann did a great short-term job for her shareholders, but may have put at risk the long-term survival of the high street stores.

*

Each year more women will rise through the ranks but for me the real heroines of the high street are those women who have created a new high street business. It was great when I went into the Emma Willis shirt shop on Jermyn Street to be greeted by the founder Emma Willis herself, who in 1999 became the first woman to open a bespoke shirt shop – invading the world of Turnbull & Asser, T.M. Lewin and Harvie and Hudson.

And it is reassuring to know that Wendy Hallett is still the driving force behind Wendy Hallett Retail.

Some successful brands take on the personality of the founder, as demonstrated by Cath Kidston whose designs achieve her objective of cheering people up. I always thought my son Edward's family had chosen a strange name for their dog when they called him Stanley, until I discovered that the terrier pictured on a lot of Cath Kidston prints was taken from her dog, also called Stanley. That cheered me up.

Some years ago, I was asked at 24 hours' notice to stand in as the guest speaker at a business award dinner. As it was to be held at the Mere Golf and Country Club, only fifteen miles from my home, I agreed. The chairman, in welcoming the guests before dinner, started by saying 'I'm afraid I have some bad news. I know how much you have been looking forward to hearing from our main speaker, but I regret to inform you that she is ill and John Timpson is taking her place.' The speaker they wanted to hear was Jacqueline Gold, chief executive of Ann Summers.

The first Ann Summers shop that opened at Marble Arch and the five that followed were simply sex shops appealing to furtive male shoppers. That all changed after the business was acquired by brothers Ralph and David Gold who turned the business into shops selling risqué lingerie, underwear, cosmetics and sex toys. In 1981 David Gold's daughter Jacqueline joined the business at the age of 21 and twelve years later, as chief executive, developed a successful business with a strong sex theme that has been able to trade in the busiest shopping centres.

Jacqueline has used her personality to develop a large female following, particularly by selling Ann Summers' products at all-women Tupperware-type parties held in the informal setting of someone's home. Jacqueline's role as a frank spokesperson for the business and ambassador for her company's products was crucial in getting Ann Summers accepted as a serious retailer.

I guess when you think about it, this would have been an almost impossible job for a man. It was OK for Jacqueline to encourage women to be more adventurous and liberated in the bedroom – any man using the same sales pitch would more likely have been seen as lecherous rather than liberating.

It is difficult to know whether Ann Summers took on the personality of Jacqueline Gold or whether Jacqueline moulded her personality to promote the business. Either way she has done a great job in creating the Ann Summers brand that now has 140 shops with a turnover of over £100m. Although profits have been patchy, Jacqueline Gold has created a most unlikely niche on many women's shopping lists.

*

Probably the most successful woman in retail is Dame Mary Perkins, whose Specsavers business made her the UK's first female self-made billionaire.

Mary's father was an optician so she followed in his footsteps, studying optometry in the 1960s at Cardiff University where she met her husband.

After university Mary took over her father's practice, in a room above a baker's shop, and soon, together with her husband Doug, opened on the high street. During the 1970s the couple grew the business to 27 shops before selling out for £2m and moving to Guernsey, where her father had lived since his retirement.

After four years away from business, Mary's interest in the world of spectacles was rekindled by the deregulation brought in by Margaret Thatcher's government. Up to then, opticians were not allowed to advertise or use promotional displays in their shops. Getting your eyes tested had no more glamour than going to the dentist.

Mary and Doug saw the opportunity and planned the future of spectacle retailing on a table tennis table in their Guernsey home. Immediately they saw how the new deregulated world would work to their advantage if they could produce welcoming shops with keen prices and punchy promotions. They put their blueprint into practice on Guernsey in 1984 and proved it worked.

For most people, living on Guernsey would have put a limit on the ability to expand, but Mary turned it to her advantage. From the start Specsavers was developed on a franchise model which they call their joint venture partnership. Potential business owners were asked to put up capital to open their store and buy into the Specsavers brand. Each store is jointly owned by the company and the independent owner. Specsavers provide all the back office support and get a percentage of turnover while the operator gets all the profit. Through franchising, Specsavers was able to grow quickly while creating a healthy cash flow.

The business model has been a spectacular success and Specsavers is now the leading brand in the UK, with a winning advertising slogan 'Should have gone to Specsavers' and the clever sponsorship of rugby league referees.

With a 35 per cent market share in the UK you might wonder whether Specsavers will run out of steam, but with franchisees providing the cash Mary Perkins has plenty of new routes for expansion. In 2002 the company diversified into the hearing aid market and for several years has been expanding overseas into Holland, Spain, Scandinavia, Australia and New Zealand. The company now has over 2,000 stores but sticks to the original principles mapped out on the table tennis table. Specsavers keeps things simple.

Specsavers is a true family business, developed by Mary and Doug, whose three children now all work in the company. With the strong cash flow guaranteed by a franchise model and no desire to splash the cash on conspicuous consumption, the family is under no pressure from banks or outside shareholders.

Dame Mary Perkins is in the proud and privileged position of having a fantastic family business to hand on to future generations.

*

Laura Ashley and her husband Bernard created the product many years before they opened their first shop in 1968. Laura Ashley's designs were the backbone of a business that changed both fashion and shop design in a similar way to Next. The Laura Ashley shops were an extension of her personality, all the merchandise and the shopfitting were clearly created by one pair of eyes, giving customers the chance to buy a coordinated wardrobe. Her shops were boldly different but the real secret of her success was her talent for creating a unique look that appealed to a wide market.

Laura's husband Bernard played a major part in developing the company and the shops relied on several thousand employees for their success, but when Laura Ashley died in 1985 after a tragic accident at the age of 60, it quickly became clear that the business had lost its core source of design flair and inspiration.

Laura Ashley's ability to develop a design theme that started with clothing and extended into home decor gave the company the opportunity to develop a big retail business that not only went from fashion to home furnishing but also spread around the world.

Laura brought a brand-new look to the high street and influenced fashion across a wide age group. After her death she left a legacy that still thrives around the world.

SPORTS SHOPS

When our children were growing up, most of their sports equipment and ski wear came from Gilberts, an independent sports shop on Water Lane, Wilmslow. If they couldn't supply what was needed we went to Monkhouse's in Cheadle Hulme, which also supplied uniform for all the local schools. Most towns had a good locally run sports shop supplied by an experienced wholesaler.

In the 1970s sports shoes became a fashion item. Trainers represented over 10 per cent of all footwear sold – reducing the demand for traditional footwear and cutting the number of shoe repair customers.

British Shoe Corporation, being in the best position to spot the new trend, launched a new chain, Olympus Sport, that provided a comprehensive range of sports clothing and equipment. The shops looked impressive and the business expanded to nearly 200 shops, many in retail parks. But British Shoe didn't talk to enough customers to discover that sports gear doesn't always sell to people who play sport. Training shoes represented a high percentage of the turnover, while the comprehensive ranges of hockey sticks, cricket bats and tennis racquets sold very slowly.

A different type of sports shop was developed by Tom Hunter in Scotland under the name Sports Division, which recognised that trainers and track suits were more likely to be worn for a walk to the pub than a workout on the training ground. When the loss-making Olympus Sport was put on the market as part of the fire sale that was about to take place at British Shoe Corporation, Tom Hunter, with the help of Philip Green and finance from the Bank of Scotland, bought Olympus in 1995 for about £20m. It was a golden opportunity: with only four Olympus stores in the same towns as Sports Division, Tom Hunter's business increased its coverage overnight from 43 to nearly 250 towns and cities. Hunter didn't waste time on market research; there was no need to analyse Olympus Sport – a few shop visits told him all he needed to know. The Olympus brand was scrapped and all the shops were converted to the Sports Division format.

Meanwhile, ex-footballer Dave Whelan was developing his own sports chain JJB, from a single shop he acquired in Wigan, after selling his first retail venture (cut-price supermarkets Whelan Discount Stores) to Ken Morrison in 1978 for £1.5 million. Dave Whelan had a similar vision to Tom Hunter with JJB selling sports clothing and footwear as a fashion item because of the appeal of well-known brands like Nike and Adidas. The biggest-selling section of stock was to become the replica football shirts, not just for fans who went to the match but for millions of others who only watched their team on television. This trend was spotted by another young entrepreneur called Mike Ashley, who started in business with a sports and ski shop in Maidenhead but went on to develop a chain of 100 shops under the Sports Soccer brand that clearly targeted the football fans.

In 1998 Tom Hunter and Philip Green decided to sell

out and agreed a deal with Dave Whelan. JJB bought Sports Division for £290m, a deal that made Tom Hunter into a multi-millionaire and set JJB on a course of highly profitable growth. By 2005, JJB had 430 substantial stores but the business faced two major problems. The first concern was how the company could satisfy the stock market by continuing to produce growing profits. JJB tried to diversify by paying Mike Ashley £5m in 2007 for the Original Shoe Company which sold upmarket branded clothing and footwear such as Timberland and Henri Lloyd. The press criticised Ashley for selling a business he had only just bought, but Ashley made a small profit on the deal and left JJB with a business they didn't understand. JJB also bought TJ Hughes, a downmarket department store chain mainly in the North-West of England that was in the words of some retail experts perhaps harshly described as 'knackered'. JJB paid £42m for TJ Hughes and were fortunate to get £56m when they sold it in a venture capital deal two years later. These two excursions outside sports retailing demonstrated the weakness of JJB's senior management, who were coming under pressure from their biggest competitor. The main problem JJB faced was the strong and aggressive tactics employed by Mike Ashley.

Mike Ashley's Sports Soccer reached 100 branches before he started trading under the name Sports World and eventually branded all his shops Sports Direct. Ashley liked collecting brands, which included Donnay, Dunlop, Slazenger, Karrimor, Kangol and Lonsdale. He must have been delighted to acquire the flagship Lillywhites shop on Regent Street, which is in sharp contrast to the direction in which Ashley took his main business.

Sports Direct sold on price. If you thought JJB were cheap

and cheerful, Sports Direct was even cheaper and shouted about their refit sales, special offers and closing down sales, with the biggest posters they could find. To me the shops looked like a jumble sale, but the customers loved them. Mike Ashley knew his market and he set about pinching business from JJB, not only by putting his prices some 15 per cent lower but also by opening shops near to the most successful JJB stores – often next door. Every new Sports Direct outlet was really bad news for JJB.

Strangely for such a secretive maverick, Ashley floated his company on the London Stock Exchange. The float went well but shareholders soon complained when Ashley (who had pocketed nearly £1bn and still had a majority stake) flouted the normal quoted company expectations. 2007 wasn't a good year to float and, as the recession started to bite, the business failed to meet its profit forecast. Faced with a stubborn chief executive producing disappointing figures, the City fell out of love with Sports Direct and at one point the shares fell from the issue price of 300p to 30p. Ashley has since proved that he knows a lot more about sports retailing than people sitting behind a City desk.

Gradually Ashley grabbed more and more of JJB's business. Dave Whelan sensibly sold his shareholding well before midnight, handing over to a disastrous spell of management by Chris Ronnie and David Jones. Ashley bought the rump of JJB out of administration, mainly to grab the stock for next to nothing and stop any competitors reopening the shops. He converted fewer than twenty JJB stores to Sports Direct. His high street battle had ended in total victory.

Mike Ashley seldom talks about his business and has never revealed his future strategy. As well as collecting a number of well-known sports brands he seems keen on taking a minority stake in other retailers. It is not clear why he became a significant shareholder in Debenhams but it was hardly surprising that he bought shares in other sports retailers Blacks Leisure and JD Sports.

With about 600 shops (after buying Allsports out of administration) JD Sport is now the only other significant sports retailer but its middle-market appeal can sit happily next to Sports Direct. It would seem unlikely that any merger between the two would ever be approved under the competition legislation and JD Sport is already controlled by Pentland, who hold 56 per cent of the equity, so you have to wonder why Ashley wants to tie up capital in his shareholding.

But Ashley often seems to defy logic. Why would a man who always tried to avoid publicity buy a football club? His ownership of Newcastle United brought him more aggravation than the grief he got from the City over the Sports Direct float. Not content with investing £150m in one football club, he then decided to mount a bid for another. You can't imagine Glasgow Rangers fans giving him an easy time.

Mike Ashley isn't the City's idea of a typical chief executive and he doesn't follow the process described as 'best practice' by business schools. He is treated with suspicion and sometimes with disrespect because he doesn't conform to convention. But his individual style, the very fact that he hasn't followed the rules, is probably one of the main reasons behind his incredible success.

If anyone wonders whether Mike Ashley deserves to be among my list of highly talented retailers they just need to note that he has created a personal fortune worth over £3bn and has the majority stake in one of the UK's most profitable retailers.

FOOD ON THE GO

If you spend a sizeable slice of your life tripping round the country visiting shopping centres (I go to over 800 of our shops every year) you can't help getting to know Greggs, McDonald's, Pret a Manger and Costa Coffee.

My most frequent lunch comes from Greggs, who must have had a series of great property directors because you can nearly always find a Greggs just when and where you need one. I was close to moving to Subway because we nearly fell out over the tomato soup. I complained about the shops that had no soup and the decision to abandon Heinz tomato soup at £1.20 in favour of homemade tomato and basil soup for £1.65. I got on first name terms with the people in their customer care department and plain tomato soup is back on the menu.

Greggs, founded first as a bakery by John Gregg in 1939, opened their first shop in Gosforth in 1951. John's son Ian, who took charge of the business after the death of his father, opened a number of shops around Tyneside before buying local chains in Glasgow, Manchester and Leeds. Each acquisition retained its trading name and was supplied by their own dedicated bakery.

In 1984 Ian Gregg moved to part-time chairman and appointed Michael Darrington as chief executive. Darrington turned the company into a national chain. His most significant move was the purchase in 1994 of Bakers Oven, a chain of over 400 outlets owned by Allied Bakeries.

During his 24 years as chief executive Michael Darrington converted all the regional chains to the Greggs fascia and turned the business from being a traditional baker's shop to a low-price takeaway cake and sandwich outlet with queues every lunchtime. Few people haven't fallen for the taste of a warm Greggs' sausage roll.

During his tenure Darrington took Greggs from a chain of 260 shops (which went public with a value of £14m) to a 1,400-branch business worth almost £400m. The company still felt like a family firm with Darrington and his executive team keeping close to their customers. Greggs have built a business out of fresh food favourites from sandwiches to sausage rolls, and steak bakes to doughnuts and ice fingers.

Darrington came to Greggs with plenty of food industry experience with United Biscuits, a modest man who turned a modest business into a match for some very high-profile competitors.

Greggs is not the most glamorous shop but with a turnover now approaching £800m from about 1,700 outlets and a market value of £1bn it is one of the shining stars of modern shopkeeping.

*

When McDonald's opened their first UK restaurant in Woolwich in 1974 I was one of their first customers, but it was a few years before McDonald's had a strong presence in the UK so most of my early McExperiences were during family camper van holidays in the USA when we regularly had hash browns and an Egg McMuffin for breakfast. In the 1980s there were enough McDonald's restaurants for me to regularly treat area managers to a Big Mac when I was spending a day visiting their shops. I also quickly discovered that McDonald's were one of the few places on the high street where you can always find a lavatory (another is any betting shop, where they also provide free little biros, but you may have to place a bet before they will give you the key to the lavatory).

After my American holidays I associated McDonald's with Drive-Thrus and out-of-town locations so was surprised that most of the early UK stores were on the high street. An easier, cheaper and quicker way to expand would have been to acquire Little Chef or the other roadside restaurant chain Happy Eater.

The original inspiration behind McDonald's and trailblazer of the fast food revolution was Ray Kroc, an American, of Czech parents, who spotted the potential when he supplied milk shake mixers to a restaurant run by Maurice and Richard McDonald in California. Impressed with the potential of their speedy service burger business, Kroc became the McDonald's franchising agent, taking ownership of the first franchise in Des Plaines, Illinois, which was an instant success.

Over the next few years Kroc bought out the founding brothers and developed the brand, the menu and the operating standards. The business was on course to become the biggest retailer in the world with a collection of McMeals that have become familiar in 35,000 restaurants around the globe. Ray Kroc had a rare combination of qualities that helped him to create a spectacular success – flair, foresight, attention to detail and a streak of ruthlessness.

Inevitably, such a big business has come in for plenty of criticism, particularly with regard to concerns about healthy eating and the exploitation of low-paid workers. Exporting the

McDonald's brand had its problems. The difficulties British retailers have in establishing their brand in the USA are similar to those encountered when attempts are made to establish proven American concepts over here.

Originally McDonald's got a warm welcome, but it was only when Jill McDonald became chief executive in 2010 that the brand moved from being a great stateside brand over here to becoming truly British. Jill McDonald looked at life through British eyes and put the customer first.

McDonald's is a Marmite business, you either love it or hate it. I have migrated to Greggs, Pret and Costa but can still be tempted by a Chicken McNugget meal.

*

Landlords will continue to be grateful for the number of coffee shops, sandwich bars and fast food outlets that still seek new shops to fulfil their expansion plans. In the 1960s when I visited our branches with my father, lunch was usually a three-course waitress-served lunch for 2/6d (12p) plus tip in a small restaurant up a flight of stairs above a shop. I looked forward to visiting our shops in Birmingham where Mitchell and Butler pubs served proper food as well as the standard pub offer of crisps, pork pie and pickled eggs.

Today there is plenty of choice. If possible I go to Costa because I like their coffee – perhaps the secret to the distinctive taste is due to the founders Sergio and Bruno Costa. The Costas sold their specialist coffee shops in 1995 to Whitbread, who have since done wonders to keep the coffee quality while expanding the chain to over 3,000 outlets around the world.

Next on my popularity list is Caffè Nero, again because I like their coffee and I can generally rely on a warmer than

average welcome from their colleagues, or baristas as they prefer to be called.

I use Starbucks if nothing else is around. For some time we
were given pure Starbucks as prescribed by Howard Schultz
in Seattle and for many years they failed to adapt the brand to
British taste. I suspect that the losses made up to 2013 were
not entirely due to shifting profits overseas to save tax – the
trading has almost certainly fallen well below expectations.
But with over 800 coffee shops in the UK they are bound to
get better and are already starting to see me as an occasional
customer.

Another US import that doesn't provide me with lunch is
Subway. I simply don't like the smell of sun-dried tomatoes,
and this was made worse for me by my first Subway experience
in Saltcoats on the west coast of Scotland where the service
was slow and unfriendly. However clever the marketing package, even a scrumptious menu can be let down by poor personal
service.

Food and drink on the modern high street goes much further than coffee shops. Domino Pizza, Pizza Express, Nandos,
Wagamamas, TGI Fridays and Jamie Oliver are helping to turn
shopping into a day out, but I'm delighted we haven't abandoned fish and chip shops and the Chinese takeaway. And
just when you thought all the pubs were closing down, along
comes Wetherspoons, inspired by Tim Martin, whose first pub
in Muswell Hill, opened in 1979, was the first of a chain of over
900 big multipurpose pubs.

*

A few years ago, when visiting our shops on the south coast
of England, I stayed the night at a hotel in Bournemouth. As

a lot of my fellow guests looked to be either over 90 years old or under nine, I decided to take the sea air, walk into town and find a place to eat. When I was a boy my grandfather had an annual holiday in Bournemouth, but he wouldn't go there now. Most of the restaurants made me feel unwelcome or uncomfortable so I finished up in Wetherspoons where I got good service and an excellent meal with plenty of interesting people-watching and a bill including beer and wine under £15.

Tim Martin is an example for other entrepreneurs to follow. He leads from the front, ignores silly rules and talks common sense. He is both a publican and a retailer, putting pubs in their proper place by providing what customers want, when they want it. I was delighted to discover that he also studied at Nottingham, my university.

Tim Martin has had the courage to change the pub industry by bringing the city centre boozer up to date, creating a pub where all ages are welcome and everyone gets personal service. Not only did he save me in Bournemouth, but a lot of his pubs now serve breakfast. Tim Martin is one of those entrepreneurs that I wish had a hand in government policy.

*

I confess, I'm prejudiced. As a regular customer and a long-time copier of so many of their best ideas, I am bound to be a big Pret a Manger fan.

The first Pret a Manger shop, a one-outlet venture in Hampstead, was a failure. The gourmet takeaway had a catchy name but within a year the business was in the hands of a liquidator. You can't therefore give credit to Jeffrey Hyman, the original creator of Pret a Manger, but some praise should go to his sister Valerie who thought up the name.

The true founders were Julian Metcalfe and Sinclair Beecham who bought the brand from the liquidator. They were fed up with poor service in tired sandwich shops selling stale bread wrapped around limp lettuce and tomato. They were on a mission to create a new lunchtime on the London high street. London in the 1980s was eager to embrace new shop concepts.

Pret a Manger was hoping to be the next niche retailing success by being the Body Shop or Tie Rack for fast food. Their first shop on Victoria Street was opened in 1986 (they put up a blue commemorative plaque 25 years later). They lost money in the first year and it took at least four years before they had honed the formula for Pret success.

Metcalfe and Beecham were not products of Procter & Gamble or graduates of a business school. They were surveyors who used passion rather than process to develop the business and focused on the simple idea of interesting fresh food with great service. When they quit the surveying and put all their time into the business, Pret started to develop.

Pret was probably helped by not being an instant success. The Pret package is a collection of great ideas put together under one roof with the same simple objectives of good fresh food and exceptional service. Today's Pret is a well-oiled machine, but if you look at the detail you see loads of little touches that no one could have visualised for the very first shop.

To retail specialists Pret a Manger is an absolute joy, a constant provider of new ideas and one of my main inspirations for change. Pret shops are so good they have encouraged lots of other businesses to get better. I have copied details from the shop design, graphics and layout, but the bit I would like to bottle for all our shops is the buzz created by the way Pret colleagues serve customers in a busy shop. Pret take pains to pick the right personalities at interview, which includes a day working in a branch with colleagues who make the final decision (it is said that only one in fourteen applicants make the grade). They are expected to give every customer a warm welcome and each week mystery shoppers check standards and give marks that make a difference to the colleagues' bonus.

It is difficult to know whether the stars of the show are the staff or the food, which is made fresh every day. When Metcalfe and Beecham opened their first shop few would have imagined that crayfish salad and avocado wraps would become top sellers.

Metcalfe and Beecham produced such a strong format that it undeniably became the most popular place to buy the office lunch, especially on a sunny summer's day when plenty of Pret packaging is taken for a picnic in the park. Having created a category killer in the capital, the constant question for the last fifteen years has been 'what should Pret do next?'

Most people were surprised when 33 per cent of the equity was sold to McDonald's in 2001. The deal was designed to give Pret the perfect partner to provide experience on how to grow, especially abroad. The cash from McDonald's gave Pret founders the chance to pursue other interests. Julian Metcalfe had already started to develop a chain of Asian-inspired fast food shops called Itsu with partner Clive Schlee. Sinclair Beecham took a step back from Pret, became a non-executive director, and put his efforts into developing a hotel.

The partnership with McDonald's didn't produce the promised profitable growth. The founders who had created the culture were no longer involved in the detail and the business missed their influence. The planned expansion into Japan ran into trouble and the Pret success story seemed to have come to a full stop.

However, Julian Metcalfe, while still building his Itsu chain, returned to Pret as creative director and Clive Schlee became chief executive. The new team brought back the old values to Pret and attracted the attention of venture capital company Bridgepoint, who took a controlling stake. Since that deal Pret has stuck to its first principles and strengthened the old culture.

Pret is now an important part of London life, but has yet to fully create the same buzz in the rest of the UK. The shops in New York are now well established and Pret are hopeful that a venture into Paris will also go well.

The incredible success in London shows the value of a strong culture delivering a great product. The next challenge is to see how far the Pret team can spread the base from their original shop in Victoria Street, London.

With so many great companies expanding their coffee bars and restaurants, the high street should always be able to fill any empty shops, and, when I visit our branches, there will always be plenty of places where I can grab something to eat.

ANTHONY PRESTON
AND MATT DAVIES

It all looks so obvious and so easy. Pets at Home has been growing for 24 years in a recession-proof business, creating lots of cash with no close competitor. Of course, if it had been that easy, someone else would have done it.

In the 1990s the big shed pet stores seemed set to be dominated by PetSmart UK, an early overseas spin-off from the PetSmart business that now has 1,350 stores in the United States, Canada and Puerto Rico. But the management team put together to develop PetSmart in the UK ran into trouble. They opened 100 stores but were running at a loss and running out of money.

This was a golden opportunity for Anthony Preston who, having found himself owning a pet food wholesaler in the 1980s, opened a pet shop in Chester in 1991. It was so successful he opened a few more, then he saw the chance of buying PetSmart in 1999.

Anthony was clearly ambitious but it was a brave move to risk the future of his healthy business by buying a basket case with three times as many shops. But Anthony knew what he was doing – the best deals are done when the seller is trading badly. PetSmart should have worked, with a proven American product, a professional team with plenty of UK retail experience and the backing of all the usual market research and consultancy advice. But in retrospect it seems Anthony Preston, whose chain had been homespun in the North-West of England, was much closer to the market. He had already discovered how pet lovers wanted to do their shopping and what they wanted to buy. He knew exactly what to do with PetSmart – they were turned into his carefully developed format – Pets at Home.

Despite taking over the only major pet chain Anthony had plenty of competitors. As well as about 7,000 independent pet shops, a large slice of the pet food trade was being creamed off by the big supermarkets, which meant that the biggest part of Pets at Home's day-to-day business had to be done on tight margins. Anthony Preston couldn't rely on the regular buyers of Pedigree Chum and Whiskas to build up his business, but with 10,000 square feet devoted to pet lovers, a Pets at Home store could cover everything from special dietary requirements to pet toys. While supermarkets concentrated on cats and dogs. Pets at Home sold everything for rabbits, snakes and goldfish. They went further by selling pets, opening Veterinary Surgeries and organising an adopt-a-pet scheme. The idea of selling live animals could be enough to deter any risk-averse retailer: one dead, undernourished hamster could lead to a public relations disaster. Alert to the danger, Pets at Home have a clear policy of putting pets before profit – comforting words when issued by head office but still dependent on the standards in each store.

When Anthony Preston decided to step down as chief executive in 2003 he chose an accountant to take his place. Matt Davies had joined Pets at Home two years earlier as Finance Director but Preston spotted that Davies had an entrepreneur's touch along with his accountancy qualifications. You'd expect a finance man to keep a tight hold on stock control and margins but Matt didn't just see Pets at Home as a set of numbers – he quickly grasped the importance of company culture.

Shortly after Preston handed over to Davies, he sold a majority of his shareholding to venture capital specialists Bridgepoint, more reason to expect a careful, process-controlled approach to any expansion plans. But Davies made the business bigger and better by choosing to put customer service as his top priority. That meant hiring colleagues who were interested in other people, and their pets.

By concentrating on the detail, searching for new parts of the pet-related market and the enthusiasm for growth that is inside every top entrepreneur, Davies made Preston's Pets At Home an even better and much bigger business.

The stores look simple and uncomplicated – dog owners to the left, cat lovers to the right and, if it is winter, the bestselling fat balls for birds piled high just inside the entrance. It seems to be based on common sense, but I'm sure the management team have had some tricky times, introduced pet products that don't sell and had periods of running fast to stand still. But the typical traumas of high street retailing seem to have been taken in their stride and Pets at Home remains the major chain for pet owners.

The strength of any company culture is tested at every change of top management or change in ownership. Over 25 years Pets at Home has had three chief executives and three owners but the change of control couldn't be detected in the stores. When Bridgepoint sold to KKR in 2010 and when Matt Davies moved to Halfords two years later, the Pets at Home success story came under the day-to-day control of Nick

Wood, who joined after a spell as chief executive of American Golf. His ownership of two dogs was, no doubt, a plus point at final interview.

Whoever holds the purse strings or runs the management team, Pets at Home knows its market, listens to its customers and delivers what they want – it sounds so easy but I'm not sure that many other people would have produced the same result.

SIR TERENCE CONRAN

It takes most retailers all their time to look after the shop. Few can combine shopkeeping with something else, but Terence Conran fitted retail into his life as a designer and restaurateur. His retailing career has influenced many well-known high street names – Hepworth, Next, Mothercare, Heals, British Home Stores, Richard Shops, the Conran Shop and most recently a design input into Marks & Spencer. But the Conran creation that has had the biggest influence was Habitat.

The first Habitat, which opened in 1964 in Fulham Road, Chelsea, shattered the mould of the existing dark brown and dull furniture shops. Habitat wasn't just a furniture shop; Conran provided a whole range of household goods all written with the same handwriting. The kitchenware was a long way from the traditional merchandise sold in department stores, ironmongers or Timothy Whites & Taylors. For the first time householders could buy bean bags, duvets and woks. Conran had already developed a new look in his original design business, mostly inspired by the time he spent travelling in Europe. The result was a shop full of coordinated design using natural materials and bright fresh colours. It was a new retail experience that immediately caught the imagination of the young homemakers.

For fifteen years Habitat enjoyed a triumphant expansion which even included an out-of-town superstore (before retail parks were developed) in Wythenshawe near to the Timpson head office. This innovative outlet opened shortly after I got married so, like a lot from our generation, the newly wed Timpsons had a Habitat home.

Inevitably the Conran furniture design dictated the look of his shops. Habitat stores were clean cut with plain white walls, a lot of natural wood and a palette of fresh colours. These design features set a standard for the rest of the high street to follow, especially chains where Conran had a direct connection, starting with Next, which was developed while Conran was Chairman of Hepworths, a role he took on in 1979.

The Hepworth job was the first of a sequence of moves that involved Conran in many different retail formats, made possible when Habitat was floated on the stock market in 1981. In 1982 Habitat merged with Mothercare, a marriage that didn't have any obvious logic other than Mothercare founder Selim Zilkha wanting to sell out and move on while Terence Conran was itching for a new challenge.

Selim Zilkha would have no doubt earned a place of his own in this book if he had stayed in UK retailing, but he took the money off to the USA where he invested $28m in an oil company which he sold for $1 billion sixteen years later.

I went to Mothercare's headquarters in about 1969 and was fascinated. The office was totally open plan with Zilkha, in full view, sitting behind his desk at the far end of this enormous room that housed everyone involved in the running of the business. This was the first time I saw computerised stock control and I thought it wonderful that a chain of shops could be automatically supplied with stock by a remote team who got daily sales data by store and by style. I was looking at the new world of retail developed by a man, Zilkha, who was at least a decade ahead of his time. (I have since discovered that it isn't always wise to hand over all these decisions to a computer.)

Conran added his design expertise to the sophisticated Mothercare stock control and the shareholders were happy. In 1983 Conran acquired Heals – a natural fit being a furniture-based department store – and later the same year bought Richard Shops from Hanson Trust.

Richard Shops had, like Timpson, been a subsidiary of UDS Group, which was bought by Hanson after a takeover bidding battle with Gerald Ronson. The Hanson plan was to strip most of the UDS assets through a series of disposals. Two main deals were being negotiated – our management buyout at Timpson and the sale of John Collier and Richard Shops to the Burton Group. Ralph Halpern, representing Burton, brought in an element of brinkmanship, tried one price chip too many and irritated James Hanson who pulled out of the deal. Attempts to secure a management buyout succeeded with John Collier but the Richard Shops team failed to get backing and Conran stepped in at the eleventh hour to add Richard Shops to his portfolio.

To Conran, Richard Shops was another Next project, a combination of good buying, clever merchandising and Habitat style design. But unlike Next, which started from scratch, Richard Shops came with a lot of baggage and before the new approach had made any major improvement to the sales performance, Conran had done another deal. In 1986 Habitat Mothercare merged with British Home Stores and became Storehouse.

British Home Stores, which became BHS, certainly needed

a makeover, whether from Conran or any other designer. It was a chain of stores without a cause. If BHS had disappeared from the high street, few people would have missed it. But Conran wasn't with Storehouse long enough to make a difference to his latest acquisition. He stepped down as chief executive in 1988, staying on as chairman for two more years before he resigned. Conran's days as a major retailer ended in 1990.

From then on Storehouse was an unhappy story. Habitat was sold in 1992 and after a series of further sales and reconstructions is now only seen as a concession inside Homebase.

In 1992 Richard Shops was sold to Sears, which itself was acquired by Philip Green in 1999. The portfolio became part of The Arcadia Group and the Richard Shops name disappeared from the high street.

The following year BHS was sold to Philip Green for £200m and Storehouse changed its name to Mothercare, which itself has had a turbulent time trying to face competition from the internet.

Perhaps it is significant that nearly all the retail companies that felt the Conran influence prospered in the 1970s and 80s, but, apart from Next, have since fallen away. The Conran look was right for a particular generation but taste has now moved on.

His lasting influence is the importance that the whole retail industry places on good, well-coordinated design. Supermarkets are now refreshing stores every seven years or so and the major shopping centre landlords demand innovative design from their tenants. We are even expected to modernise shoe repair shops, which is fine as long as no one thinks that pretty-looking shops are more important than having shopkeepers with charisma who can give a personal service.

DEAN BUTLER

In the early 1990s, I was so intrigued by the new chain, Vision Express, I managed to arrange a visit to their Nottingham head office and met their boss.

Dean Butler worked in the USA at Procter & Gamble for fourteen years until he stumbled on his big idea. Talking to a friend with ophthalmic training, Dean discovered that the manufacture of new lenses is relatively uncomplicated. So simple in fact, he decided to leave Procter & Gamble and create opticians that promised to produce new glasses within an hour. This clear goal became the key driver behind LensCrafters, with the first shop near Cincinnati airport. Within five years there were over 200 branches and today the chain is approaching 1,000. Three years into the project Dean sold his shareholding to the US Shoe Corporation and after two years as President left the company to start Vision Express in the UK.

In creating the one-hour service Dean changed the whole concept of an optician. Instead of providing a service for patients, LensCrafters were catering for customers. It didn't take long for Dean to discover that sales dramatically increased wherever he had really good sales people talking to customers. And with the lens-making process now being fairly straightforward he was able to develop a system that was easy to teach to any willing recruit. Dean decided that rather than recruiting qualified opticians, it was better to find people with a positive personality and give them the specialised LensCrafters training.

He was so confident that these raw recruits could deliver an accurate service, he dressed the company-trained opticians in white coats and put the production laboratory in the shop window. To keep his critical one-hour promise the colleagues only collected a bonus on those jobs that were completed within an hour.

In 1988 Dean opened the first UK Vision Express store in the Metro Centre near Gateshead. If anything, his concept worked even better over here and it was one of the top three UK opticians when Dean did a deal with Grand Optical, based in France, which gave him his exit. In my view, though, this signalled the end of some of the magical touches that helped Dean achieve such an instant success.

It was a brilliant example of invention, clear thinking and simplicity, and, a real plus for me, it was a service business, so there were plenty of examples for us to follow.

My hour at the Vision Express head office taught me so much I invited Dean to come to talk to our next area managers' conference.

In the early 1990s we had just over 200 shops and our field team met in the dining room at our home, which is where Dean had them spellbound while, for over an hour, he talked commercial common sense.

I particularly remember their eyes lighting up when Dean talked about Canada. 'We had a shop in every possible town and city so for the next year I stopped investing money and set the team a simple target. I told them to make sure they had a great manager in every branch. We easily had the best year ever.' That advice still applies today to every shop, store or supermarket.

I asked Dean to stress the importance of customer service and he could not have put over a stronger message. 'My experience', he said, 'is that the way customers are treated is the main factor that determines whether they will come back to buy more. It makes a big difference if you welcome every customer within 30 seconds of entering the shop, but don't be overbearing – you are there to help. Word of mouth', he continued, 'is the best form of advertising and the best way to impress is to settle a complaint. Dissatisfied customers can be turned into your biggest fans.'

In retrospect the biggest bonus I got from Dean's experience was the idea of putting the star performers in the shop window. By having white-coated opticians operating in full view of every customer he both demonstrated confidence in their expertise and promoted their service. I did the same when we introduced watch repairs into Timpson and it made a mammoth difference. More recently we have put our photo gift workshop into the window of every Max Spielmann photo shop with similar success. It helps to listen to other people's ideas, especially when your mentor is Dean Butler.

It was great to meet a fellow thinker who had the confidence to ignore 'best practice' and trust his judgement. Dean Butler gave us the faith to follow our instinct and to believe in common sense.

RICHARD TOMPKINS

L ike a lot of lively entrepreneurs Richard Tompkins didn't totally switch off when he was on holiday. During vacation in Chicago in 1958, he spotted that Sperry & Hutchinson's Green Stamps were becoming a popular feature with American shoppers. Tompkins, whose printing business was a world away from retailing, bought the rights to use the Green Shield name from a luggage manufacturer and set about copying all he had seen on holiday by developing the Green Shield Stamp trading company in the UK.

It worked, mainly because of the extensive catalogue which showed a wide range of luxury goods and household items from corkscrews to top-of-the-range televisions. The more expensive items could only be claimed after collecting an enormous number of stamps, but the fact they were available at all sent shoppers to places where the stamps were on offer. A careful look at the purchases needed to collect enough stamps to qualify for a luxury three-piece suite would have put off anyone with any sense, but Green Shield had such a psychological appeal customers sought out shops that offered stamps.

In effect Tompkins was making two margins – a profit on goods from the catalogue and a fee from the retailer – but the best margin was made out of collectors who never cashed in their stamps. There was no shortage of companies wanting to join the scheme, with the biggest users of Green Shield Stamps being petrol stations and Tesco.

Tompkins gained a lot by getting in first. Other stamp companies followed, including Sperry & Hutchinson, who, having had the green stamp hijacked, opted for pink. But, with the public already fondly filling books with green stamps, the pink ones seemed a poor copy and never matched Tompkins's scheme, although Pink Stamps were widely used as a tax-saving way of paying commission and bonuses to company employees. In the 1960s when Pink Stamps were offered to Timpson shoe shop assistants instead of the normal cash incentive, the management team misunderstood the maths and gave away so many stamps our colleagues were able to furnish half their houses and Timpson finished with an enormous bill from Sperry & Hutchinson.

I was intrigued by the big Green Shield redemption shop that opened in Wilmslow, my home town at the time. The centre was one of many around the country, catering for customers who wanted to exchange their stamps for merchandise. It was strange to see a new type of shop that couldn't have existed ten years earlier.

As the trend gathered pace the stamps were used as a major marketing tool with double and even triple stamp days proving popular with the public. What seemed set to be a permanent feature of retailing was stopped in its tracks overnight by Tesco's 'Operation Checkout'. In a dramatic move, Tesco's recently appointed new boss Ian MacLaurin scrapped the stamps and replaced them with price cuts which stole a march on all the competition. It was the beginning of a rapid slide and, once petrol stations started pulling out, the writing was on the wall for Tompkins and his Green Shield Stamps.

But Tompkins took a simple and brilliant step by converting his redemption depots into retail shops where anything in the catalogue could be bought for cash. Another holiday, this time in Greece, gave Tompkins a name for this new retail format – his retail catalogue shops were rebranded Argos (after the Greek city) in 1973.

I never exchanged a book of stamps in the Wilmslow store but, almost as soon as it became Argos, I was sent there with a list to help with the Christmas shopping. I couldn't get in the door – the queue had spilled over to the pavement outside. It took an hour before I was at the counter filling in my order with one of those useful little biros that these days I pick up from the bookmakers.

Argos was a great success – one suspects a lot better than the Green Shield Stamps that helped to create a category of store half-way between traditional shopping and mail order. After Argos had been running for six years Tompkins sold it to British American Tobacco (BAT) and completed a magical retail adventure. He introduced a novel promotional tool to the UK; when it faced a rapid fall in favour he reinvented the business by creating a new type of shopping; and then six years later had the courage to ignore the temptation to continue to enjoy success and sold out for a good price (£35m) at the age of 61, assured of a pretty good pension.

JULIAN RICHER

I'm not the slightest bit interested in hi-fi or sound systems, but when I was on holiday on the Isle of Lewis in 1996 and started to read Julian Richer's book *The Richer Way* I was fascinated. I am not surprised that Julian had to publish the book himself. As I know from experience, it is tough trawling around publishing houses and being rejected by commissioning editors who want business books that conform with the practice preached at business schools. As a result most business books are written by academics or consultants and despite a fancy cover with a catchy title are filled with familiar theory backed up with little practical experience. Julian's book couldn't be more different. It tells the story of a hands-on retailer who has invented a unique and highly successful business by doing everything in his own way. I was so delighted to find a book full of fresh ideas I started listing the ones I wanted to copy and returned from holiday full of plans to put a bit of *The Richer Way* into Timpson.

Julian, like a lot of natural entrepreneurs, started doing business at an early age – selling hi-fi equipment when he was still at school. By the time he reached 17, he had three people working for him and two years later opened his first shop at London Bridge. That shop set the format for all further Richer branches to follow.

Julian picked cheeky, slightly off-pitch positions at modest rents but drew in the customers with bold promotions advertising unbeatable prices ('We will beat any competitor by up to £100!'). I can't think of any other business that has made such a success of this technique. Julian has created his own style of retailing and turned it into a fabulous format. So much so, the original London Bridge store has appeared in the *Guinness Book of Records* for over twenty years for having the highest sales per square foot of any shop in the world.

No one can claim to have been more hands-on than Julian. If a customer sends in a complaint they get a personal reply and if any of his 500 colleagues want to see Julian he will make himself available. Julian brought in the personal touch for every new recruit by holding his residential induction course at his home. It's a powerful way to show how the owner's philosophy is so central to the business. Julian hasn't just built a business on clever property deals (he owns as many of the freeholds as he can) and smart bulk buying to ensure his ability to promote the best deals. His single-minded culture is based on giving customers a great service by picking great people to run his shops.

Few retailers do more to look after their colleagues. Probably the biggest bonus of working for Richer Sounds is that, whoever you are in the company, the boss and owner knows who you are – a very important feature in a company where all management appointments are made from within the company.

Julian set the gold standard for company perks by buying a number of company holiday homes where colleagues stay for free, and famously lending star performers a Rolls Royce to drive for a week as a reward for coming top of the sales league.

Julian believes in carrying on a constant dialogue with

customers through service questionnaires and with colleagues who actively use the company suggestion scheme in the knowledge that they are guaranteed a cash reward for every idea.

Any company that is looking for some new employee perks might find that the perfect idea is already in place at Richer Sounds where free massage sessions and a take-your-pet-to-work scheme is on the list. We at Timpson have not only copied the idea of holiday homes, we bought one of the Richer Sounds villas in Spain when we launched a similar scheme (keeping ahead of the game, Julian replaced that villa with somewhere even better!).

My son James also copied the Richer idea of inviting colleagues to training courses at his house and taking them out on a long country walk before lunch at a local pub. He finds it a great way of getting to know the young rising stars in the business.

You won't find Richer Sounds on the busiest high streets or in any out-of-town shopping centres but gaudy posters advertise their presence in some of the most unlikely places. The Richer marketing style is very much in your face – blunt statements in big letters. Price offers are the headline but everything is underwritten by the promise of excellent service and a high degree of honesty. Richer gives the strong impression that he is on the customers' side and that bigger businesses and government regulations aren't going to get in his way.

We, at Timpson, have tried to emulate the strength of Richer's philosophy and have copied some of his ideas but we don't match the disciplined way he has never been tempted to stray from the original format. It can't have been easy to stick to first principles against new competition from the big retailers and the internet. As a result Julian Richer has only grown to 53 shops but has 100 per cent control and a strong freehold portfolio.

There are, no doubt, other retailers, like us, who have pinched a bit of *The Richer Way* and have every reason to be grateful for the example we have followed. Julian has no children to take on the business so has shrewdly decided to leave the business to a trust owned and run by its employees. That gives Richer Sounds a much better chance of surviving for a few more decades. If the business were sold and control handed over to a professional manager, the new regime would soon be bewildered by Julian's way of making money and within a matter of months the magic would disappear.

GERALD RATNER

Many people may wonder why my list includes someone so well known for making a big mistake. On 23 April 1991 Gerald Ratner made his speech to the Institute of Directors, which included two jokes: 'We do cut glass sherry decanters complete with six glasses on a silver-plated tray your butler can serve you drinks on, all for £4.99. People say how can you sell this for such a low price? I say because it is total crap.' He went on: 'We even sell a pair of gold earrings for under £1, which is cheaper than a prawn sandwich from Marks & Spencer, but I have to say the sandwich will probably last longer than the earrings.'

That speech brought the *Sun* headline 'ROTNERS', cost him his job and rocked the Ratners share price. His misfortune taught us all a lesson. It is dangerous to make a joke of your own business.

But in the seven years that led up to his faux pas, Gerald Ratner had shown the rest of the jewellery world how to make money and taught a few tricks to the rest of us on the high street.

At the age of 34 Ratner took on the management of a family business with just over 100 shops at the value end of the jewellery trade. With an aggressive approach to pricing and brash displays he made Ratners' shops a stark contrast to their staid and conventional competitors. His low-price tickets, fluorescent display posters and bags of bling at the front of the window appealed to customers who were reluctant to enter a traditional jeweller's. Ratners found a new market, attracting lots of lower income customers, particularly people under 40. A new retail star was born and when he made a bid for the 450-shop rival H. Samuel, their shareholders gave him a warm welcome. Gerald Ratner was on a roll. For five years he pursued his cut-price technique and progressively acquired the major multiples including Watches of Switzerland, Leslie Davies and the more upmarket Ernest Jones. In two years the Ratners share price rose from 27p to £4.20.

Not content with dominating the mass market UK jewellery trade, Ratner was one of the few UK retailers to make a successful invasion of the United States through his acquisition of Kays. In six years he had built a 2,500-shop business (1,500 in the UK, 1,000 in the USA) with profits reaching £125m.

As trading got tougher towards the end of the 1980s Ratner brought in even bolder price promotions including a mammoth sale that started four weeks before Christmas. It was so successful he ran an even bigger sale the next year and had queues of customers keen to pick up the biggest bargains.

Cut-price promotion can become a drug and Gerald Ratner was hooked. Christmas 1991 was tough for all retailers and Ratners found it trickier than most. They took even deeper discounts but this time the pre-Christmas sales failed to attract enough customers. With sales down and margins squeezed, profits suffered.

It is possible that Ratner's aggressive pricing ploy did as much damage as the 'crap' remark. Whatever the reason, Ratner's reputation was in ruins. Gerald lost his job, any Ratners shops were changed to H. Samuel and the group was renamed Signet.

But, in an amazing period during the 1980s, Gerald Ratner completely changed the face of our multiple jewellers.

THE UNSUNG HEROES

This book is full of bold entrepreneurs who have shaped
UK shopping over the last 50 years and more. But it would
be incomplete without recognising those brilliant hands-on
retailers who serve shoppers so well on a daily basis that their
customers keep coming back for more.

I am pleased to single out some of the exceptional retailers
I have discovered from personal experience. They show that
you don't have to run 300 shops or produce £200m turnover
before being named as a great retailer.

One day I was driving to our office on the M56 when I
got stuck in the usual traffic jam. The guy driving the car on
my right signalled at me to wind my window down. 'Like the
shirt', he said, 'bet it came from David's place in Hoole.' He
was right – my wife Alex had bought it from Grooms in Hoole
near Chester and given it to me for Christmas. Grooms isn't
on a busy high street but their distinctive styling has a wide
following.

*

The nearest shop to my house is amazing. I have watched The
Hollies Farm Shop grow from a modest barn selling produce
to passers-by and customers staying on their caravan park
into today's multimillion-pound-turnover business. Each year

something new is created – a restaurant, a deli, a gift shop, a butchers and freezer cabinets full of the innovative COOK ready meals. The temptation to buy more of the luxury snacks than you intended has earned The Hollies the nickname 'the 50 pound shop', but the top end prices of their products don't stop the shop being busy every time I visit.

*

Another superb retailer hides down Heyes Lane in Alderley Edge nearly half a mile away from the main shopping street. Percy Grantham, named after the grandfather of Michael who, with his family, now runs the shop, is an amazing delicatessen where you can find the best selection of cheeses and cold meats in the North-West of England. The shop hasn't changed much since I discovered it in the 1970s but Michael and his family just make their produce better and better as the years go by. Percy Granthams is a true centre of excellence.

*

An example of great retailing is Party Places in Ellesmere Port where you can hire fancy dress for functions with any theme you care to mention. Three floors of costumes cater for kids' parties as well as adults faced with finding something to wear for a Caribbean evening, a 60s night, or a party where you have to dress as someone who is dead and famous. They have a treasure trove of outfits and accessories but it isn't just the wide range of stock that makes Party Places a great shop – it is the helpful, knowledgeable and happy staff who make the difference. They make shopping fun.

*

The retail icons who build up big businesses get the headlines but their success can only be created with the help of superb shopkeepers who deal with the day-to-day business. I have seen the difference a really good manager can make at Timpson. Bob Northover who has managed our Taunton branch for over fifteen years has nurtured so many loyal customers the shop takes three times the turnover we would expect from the town. Go there and you are entertained by the friendly banter, come back and Bob will remember who you are. Andy Konis who runs the Timpson shop on the King's Road in Chelsea has, just like Bob, developed a devoted clientele by giving great service, as has Ricky Bickell in Petty Cury, Cambridge; and there are loads more like them around the country.

While the boss sets the strategy and does the deals that determine future success, there will always be some key managers who make sure the organisation delivers the right service to customers. We would never have turned round Max Spielmann without the inspirational leadership of Sue Burden who oversees a chain of 350 outlets by the sheer force of her personality. Perry Watkins, who has the same role for nearly 900 Timpson shops, has an uncanny knack of recruiting the personalities we need and somehow makes sure, despite having many shops that are staffed by only one person, that they are all open on time every day.

These miracle-workers deserve to be praised alongside the well-known names that are listed in my retailing hall of fame.

MY TOP 50

50 Michael Darrington

During his 24 years as chief executive, Michael Darrington found a way to fight off the supermarkets that closed down most of the high street bakers and transformed Greggs into the nation's favourite provider of a snack lunch. When he joined, Greggs had 260 shops, mostly north of Birmingham – seven regional chains with local management and separate brand names. Today all 1,650 shops have the Greggs fascia and sell the same much-loved doughnuts and sausage rolls from Falkirk to Folkestone. Thanks to Michael Darrington every Timpson shop has a local Greggs where I can buy lunch.

49 Jacqueline Gold

With a turnover of just over £100m from 140 shops Ann Summers isn't that big and isn't particularly profitable, but it's a company with attitude that brings spice and variety to the high street. That attitude is provided by Jacqueline Gold, who had the inspiration to turn Ann Summers into a Tupperware-type party and has shown how much a business can be shaped by the personality of the boss.

48 Gerald Ratner

The inclusion of Gerald Ratner on my list will come as a surprise to those who only associate him with an ill-judged speech to the Institute of Directors. But before that notorious event Gerald Ratner had turned his 130-store family business into the biggest jewellery retailer in the world with 2,500 shops. He was bold, ambitious and innovative, using aggressive marketing to put jewellery shopping within everyone's budget. Few people have had as much influence on the shape of our high street.

47 Jim McCarthy

Jim McCarthy of Poundland appears on my list to represent a new breed of discount retailers alongside Home Bargains, Poundworld, Poundstretcher and B&M Bargains. After a career that took him to Dillons, T&S Stores and Sainsbury's, Jim McCarthy found his perfect role as chief executive of Poundland. He totally understood what customers want from a discount store and helped Poundland become the first of these new discount chains to float on the London Stock Market.

46 Barbara Hulanicki

Barbara Hulanicki's Biba didn't last long but was around long enough to shift consumer power in favour of fashion followers in their teens and twenties. Biba in Kensington broke all the rules of shopkeeping and created a store that suited the 60s generation so well it set a new standard for other retailers to follow. My wife, Alex, lived in London between 1963 and 1966 so I asked whether she went to Biba. She gave me the withering look that meant I'd asked a stupid question. 'Of course', Alex replied. 'Everyone did.'

45 Roger Bromley

Roger Bromley, great-grandson of the founder of Russell & Bromley, is here to represent the family members who have cleverly managed the business since 1880.

Russell & Bromley has shown the benefits that come from consistent management by successive generations of a family business. The Bromleys continue to prosper long after nearly every other shoe shop and most other retailers have gone out of business.

Roger Bromley has a faithful following of loyal customers because his shops religiously maintain a high level of taste, quality and service.

44 Anthony Preston

Anthony Preston saw an opportunity that no one else spotted, turned around a business that others had found difficult to run and created a company that seems so simple we all wonder why we didn't do it ourselves.

Pets at Home has been a seamless success story since Anthony Preston bought PetSmart in 1999. His timing and judgement have been faultless. After stepping back from day-to-day management he helped the business to become even bigger by choosing Matt Davies, now running Tesco UK, as his successor and using two venture capital deals to build a chain of nearly 400 stores that floated in 2014 with a market value of £1.2bn.

43 Tom Farmer

In making Kwik Fit the market leader, Tom Farmer not only created a billion-pound business, he also showed the rest of us in service retailing how to make shop floor colleagues stars of the business. A clear corporate image, strongly reflected in the mechanics' overalls and promoted by the slogan 'You can't get better than a Kwik Fit fitter', put the people who served the public in pride of place.

Other service retailers should follow Tom Farmer's example – publicise the people who do the job and make sure there is a great team in every branch.

42 Terence Conran

Habitat changed the look of our homes and the way we lived. Terence Conran showed us how to be part of the 60s revolution by filling our houses with simple but stylish wooden furniture, bright coloured accessories and beanbags. Conran triggered a new look for shops and, as chairman of Hepworth, was one of the instigators of Next. While developing the Storehouse Group he also oversaw changes at Mothercare, Richard Shops, Heals and British Home Stores.

Conran designs were perfect through the 1960s and 70s, but by the millennium fashion had moved on and most of Conran's Storehouse chains have now disappeared, though Next has gone on to be a retail giant.

41 Terry Leahy

Ian MacLaurin picked his successor Terry Leahy as the man to increase market share in the UK and grow globally.

Terry Leahy fulfilled his promise by increasing UK market share from 20 per cent to over 30 per cent and expanding to over 3,000 stores overseas.

Terry Leahy turned Tesco from a very big business into a giant, building enormous Tesco Extras, with the space to expand way beyond the core food offer into clothing, electricals, mobile phones and banking.

Despite this success, Tesco wasn't without its problems. Fresh & Easy in California never made money and the British public resented relentless growth at home, but the big head office team was still in arrogant mood when Terry Leahy picked Philip Clarke as his successor.

This relatively low placing on my list is influenced by what has happened since Terry Leahy left Tesco. Either he picked the wrong successor or he selected the right man but left him with a load of problems. He created a big business but it remains to be seen whether it got too big.

40 Bernard Lyons

If Bernard Lyons' bold bid for Burtons in 1965 had been successful he would have controlled over 25 per cent of the menswear market with John Collier, Alexandre Ltd, Burton and Jackson the Tailor. It isn't surprising that the bid was rejected by the Monopolies and Mergers Commission.

Despite the difficulties in the early 80s, which I observed when Timpson was a UDS subsidiary, Bernard Lyons showed great skill in building up such a diverse group that included Richard Shops, Allders and the Duty Free shops at Heathrow airport.

On a personal level Bernard Lyons took a big gamble when

he asked me to run Swears & Wells, the smallest chain in the Group. Two years later that decision led to an unexpected invitation to return to Timpson and run our family business, so I have a lot to thank him for.

39   Mark Fenwick

Mark is here to represent his family, who have patiently developed the Fenwick chain of department stores since 1882 when his great grandfather opened a shop in Northumberland Street, Newcastle.

Other family department stores either expanded too quickly or got stuck in the past but Fenwicks has made slow but spectacular progress. In 1891 they took a bold move by buying premises in Bond Street but the next really big deal didn't happen until 110 years later when they bought Bentalls.

By keeping their standards of quality and service up to date the Fenwick family have retained the trust of their customers and kept control of their business for over 130 years.

38   Dean Butler

Dean Butler is on my list because he taught me so much about service retailing. I was instantly impressed when he described how he developed LensCrafters in the USA and then used the concept to bring Vision Express to the UK. I have never forgotten his story about having a record year in his Canadian business by concentrating on having a great manager in every shop. I also remember him saying that Vision Express didn't employ opticians, they looked for people with personality who they would train to make spectacles.

His other winning technique was to put the craftsmen in the shop window.

All these ideas have worked really well at Timpson.

37 Julian Richer

Julian Richer rewrote the rules of retailing by building a business well away from the prime sites. Some analysts say that the priorities for every shopkeeper are location, location, location. Julian Richer has proved them wrong.

He has developed a great business that attracts customers with amazing service by picking the right colleagues and looking after them with an inspiring range of benefits.

Richer's shops can teach good retailing to other shopkeepers. At Timpson, we have copied many Richer Sounds ideas. Some seemed far-fetched, like the holiday homes and holding company conferences at his house, but try them out and you quickly discover Julian Richer has built his business by finding a lot of wacky ideas that work.

36 Graham Kirkham

Furniture stores are about as far removed from shoe repairing as windsurfing is from knitting, but I still feel qualified to admire the way Graham Kirkham turned a small furniture company, DFS, into a billion-pound business.

Like a lot of my heroes Graham Kirkham is a natural retailer, running his business by instinct. He found it easy to motivate his team and bring in the customers, showing that good retailing isn't produced by a process, it is a product of flair, great people and common sense.

35 Arthur Ryan

Arthur Ryan, an unfamiliar name to many other retailers, is the man who developed one of the biggest recent game changers on the high street, Primark.

Founded in Dublin, as a development for Associated British Foods, Arthur Ryan delivered a business way beyond their expectations. It took some years before Primark blossomed but when the closure of Littlewoods, C&A and Woolworths opened up the opportunity, Primark became a massive new force in retailing.

34 Laura Ashley

Laura Ashley shops oozed the personality of their creator. She developed her style of fabrics into a range of fashion and home furnishing that always bore her individual stamp.

Laura Ashley used her flair to give customers a rare combination of style, quality and value that appealed to a wide cross section of consumers. She also showed other retailers how to turn a designer brand into a mass market multiple. Her influence raised design standards throughout retailing.

33 David Alliance

In a career during which he created one of the biggest textile businesses in the world, David Alliance also played a major part in mail order shopping.

N Brown Group plc, and its subsidiary JD Williams, has consistently catered for specialist sections of the market by giving them a selection of merchandise that is not readily available on the high street.

While other mail order catalogues have amalgamated, N Brown has remained independently true to its original principles which are now being applied to internet shopping.

32 Geoff Mulcahy

Most people associate Woolworths with its final failure, but several years earlier, Geoff Mulcahy turned an ailing Woolworths into a City success story.

By making Woolworths part of the Kingfisher Group, Mulcahy could use the cash from selling off Woolworth properties to turn B&Q into the market leader in a growing DIY sector. Kingfisher also acquired Comet, Screwfix and Superdrug and became such a big retailer Geoff Mulcahy got close to pulling off one of the biggest deals for decades before a last-minute intervention by Walmart prevented the proposed merger between Kingfisher and Asda.

Once Asda walked away, Geoff Mulcahy started breaking up Kingfisher, a job he did with the same skill that had saved Woolworths twenty years earlier.

31 Philip Green

I was part of a consortium that spotted the potential of doing a leveraged buyout of Sears Holdings. We never put the deal together, but three years later Philip Green did, and was on the way to building the UK's biggest private retail business.

British Home Stores (renamed BHS) provided Philip Green with plenty of personal cash but was never a showcase for his retailing skills. The purchase of Arcadia was much better suited to his flair for fashion and publicity. To his credit Philip Green has used his celebrity status to provide practical help to young people hoping for a career in fashion and retail.

30 Tim Martin

With an increasing amount of retail sites being occupied by caterers, it is entirely appropriate that Tim Martin is included on my list.

Tim Martin has used customer-focused common sense to turn Wetherspoons from a chain of pubs into an all-day food and drinks outlet serving more meals than any restaurant chain and pouring more coffees than Pret a Manger.

By changing the way to run a pub, Tim Martin is turning public houses into retail premises and helping to attract more consumers to traditional high streets.

29 Patrick Farmer

Patrick Farmer was a non-executive director of Timpson from 1994 until 2012, so I know his retail credentials from personal experience. He not only gave me the wisdom gained from a lifetime in retail, he also taught me that you can run a great business and still be perfectly charming and polite in the process. But his inclusion in my list is not prompted by his time at Timpson.

Patrick Farmer, with his brother Tim, ran their family chain of shoe shops, John Farmer, and after that became part of Clarks they also controlled Ravel. They consistently outperformed the rest of us running shoe shops and I still can't understand why Clarks asked Patrick to run Clarks

International, when he was the ideal candidate to mastermind the amalgamation of Peter Lord, K Shoe Shops, Clarks and John Farmer.

He would have done an awesome job.

28 George Davies

As the central figure in creating Next, George Davies set a new standard for fashion retailing. Suddenly shops selling clothes from circular metal rails looked old-fashioned and customers started to demand the chance to choose a complete matching outfit in one shop.

George Davies was full of new ideas – Next for Men, Next Interiors, Next Directory, Next to Nothing, followed by 'George' and 'Per Una'.

The near collapse of Next under his control is evidence that George Davies is more talented at coming up with fantastic ideas than putting them into practice, but he set the scene that other successful retailers have followed.

27 Mary Perkins

Few customers at their 2,000 optical shops and not many of the millions who are familiar with their advertising slogan 'Should have gone to Specsavers' realise that the company was founded and is still run and owned by a woman who is now over 60 and lives on Guernsey.

Mary Perkins spotted the opportunity when Margaret Thatcher's government deregulated the spectacle business. Being based in Guernsey, Mary expanded through a version of franchising that she called joint venture partnerships.

Few chains are as big as Specsavers and it is still a family business.

26 Philip Harris

Philip Harris has been called the best carpet retailer in the world. He created two carpet chains, Harris Queensway and Carpetright, which were so successful he turned them into two fortunes.

Like a lot of people on my list he was already learning the business when most of his contemporaries were still concentrating on school. It is difficult for a business college to match that sort of experience.

He was born into one of the most difficult sectors within retailing. Only a true genius could become king of the carpet shops.

25 Allan Leighton and Archie Norman

Since Allan Leighton famously announced he was 'going plural' he has been involved with a wide spread of retailers from Selfridges to the Post Office (which during his watch was still part of Royal Mail). In all these roles he has come across as a clear thinker but the job that secured his inclusion in my list was at Asda, where he was half of a double act with Archie Norman.

The Leighton/Norman partnership saved Asda by putting people first and bringing a bit of show business into the stores. They concentrated on what their customers wanted and recognised the vital part their store colleagues played in delivering a great service.

They learnt a lot from supermarkets in the USA where they found the greeters, company huddle and big colleague badges – stateside showbiz that put a special buzz into Asda, with ideas that have been copied in many other UK retailers.

24 Malcolm Walker

Malcolm Walker is another of my top 50 retailers who has come back and proved that his first success wasn't a fluke. After a period in the wilderness he returned to run Iceland and repeated his success.

An instinctive shopkeeper, Malcolm Walker ignores the rules of retailing best practice and does things his way, never afraid to try new ideas that give Iceland customers a better deal.

One thing they preach at business school is to 'keep it simple'. Sadly not enough MBAs put that bit of advice into practice. Malcolm Walker does, which is one of the main reasons why he has been so successful.

23 Andy Street

Since the recession started in 2008 John Lewis, under the guidance of Andy Street, has built more stores, increased sales, made more money and improved its reputation. The success of John Lewis's Click and Collect service is showing others how to make money out of internet shopping.

Andy Street has used his dynamic personality to lead by example. He is a visible character to the partners, the customers and the commentators. He is one of the retail trade's best communicators, recognising the power of public relations and the contribution the John Lewis Christmas TV advertisement makes to their public image.

22 Mike Ashley

Press coverage concentrates on Mike Ashley's eccentric, publicity-shy business style and his apparent contempt for shareholders who want a more conventional approach to governance. But not enough is said about the remarkable way Mike Ashley has taken sports retailing by the scruff of the neck and obtained a stranglehold on the market.

He smothered the competition, particularly JJB Sports, by deep discounts and dramatic sales that sold the cheapest stock, in bold shops that he put as near to his competitors as possible.

To the casual observer Sports Direct looks like a market stall for football supporters, but look a bit deeper and you will find a slick, well-planned operation.

If you look beyond the eccentricity you find Mike Ashley is a fantastically successful shopkeeper who is worth careful study – other retailers could learn a lot.

21 Harry Levison

Although much of the credit is given to Charles Clore, Harry Levison built British Shoe Corporation, which in the 1970s and 80s had nearly 30 per cent of the UK footwear market.

He was a brilliant shoe buyer, building a team that produced ranges targeted at all sections of the shoe market from Saxone and Dolcis to Freeman Hardy Willis and Curtess, supported from an enormous shoe warehouse in Braunstone near Leicester.

There has never been such a dominant collection of multiple shops, put together through Charles Clore's takeover tactics but made to work by Harry Levison's genius.

20 Julian Metcalfe

Julian Metcalfe's Pret a Manger set a new standard for fast food retailers. The products and service are so good it is one of the few British brands that have succeeded in New York. I will even walk past my favourite Greggs to go to Pret, it is that good.

Julian Metcalfe built a fantastic branch network in London by knowing how to pick the right site for Pret customers, but the real secret is having a range of fresh quality food served by switched-on colleagues who can cope with the busiest lunchtime crowds.

Not content with creating one leading food chain, Julian Metcalfe is also developing the Asian-inspired Itsu, which is already serving over 10 million customers a year.

19 Jack Cohen

When Jack Cohen opened his first shop he could not have anticipated that it would grow into such a big business, but, judging by the pace with which he acquired more shops, it might have been his ambition.

Within eight years he had 100 shops and twenty years later Tesco had grown to 800 outlets. He used his market trading experience to concentrate on low-price goods, boldly displayed. He was a consumer champion, giving customers what they wanted at prices everyone could afford.

Tesco has moved a long way from the original shops with counter service and piles of stock, but it was Jack Cohen who founded one of the biggest retailers in the world.

18 Montague Burton

Montague Burton opened over 600 shops and claimed that Burton was the biggest chain of multiple tailors in the world. But he wasn't just an innovative retailer, he made as much money out of property and manufacturing.

The business was almost entirely based on made-to-measure suits that were made in Burton's own factories. As well as owning the production Montague Burton owned the freehold of a lot of his shops. Like many multiples that grew in the 1930s the balance sheet was boosted by a valuable property portfolio, many of which were built for the Burton business.

By 1990 the business no longer sold made-to-measure suits and the Burton factories were closed, but the freehold portfolio acquired by Montague Burton played an important part in reshaping the high street.

17 Stanley Kalms

Stanley Kalms demonstrated how to adapt to changes in consumer demand.

Dixons started out as a camera shop, but, unlike Jessops, which has stuck to photography, the company has developed its product in line with the pace of technology.

Stanley Kalms had the knack of making the right moves at the right time. He not only had the eye to spot an opportunity, he also had the courage to go for it.

He diversified his camera shops into the electrical business, then made a major move by buying Currys and cleverly moved much of the business out of town.

Business students wanting to learn about long-term business development should study the career of Stanley Kalms.

16 Harry Gordon Selfridge

It must have taken a lot of courage for a 50-year-old American to spend £400,000 in the 1900s building an enormous department store in London. Harry Gordon Selfridge (called Harry by his family and friends) turned his investment into an amazing business by hands-on management and attention to detail.

Harry Selfridge already had 24 years of experience in Chicago department stores, where he had a reputation for enthusiasm and relentless innovation. He was a showman and a self-publicist who put fun into retailing. He emphasised the importance of customer service and felt shopping should be entertaining.

He ran Selfridges for 30 years and although the company struggled after the 1931 depression (when Harry Selfridge was 75) and he spent his last few years heavily in debt, he still left a fantastic legacy which remains one of the top stores in the world.

15 Isaac Wolfson

If Isaac Wolfson hadn't been employed as a merchandiser at Great Universal Stores the business would probably have gone bust.

Within two years Isaac Wolfson was in charge and under his guidance the company became one of Europe's three largest mail order companies and had a diverse portfolio of over 2,000 multiple shops.

For 60 years GUS was managed by the Wolfson family while keeping as little contact as possible with shareholders, merchant bankers, City analysts and journalists. To keep tight control most shares in issue had no vote.

Under Wolfson management GUS profits grew for 48 consecutive years. One wonders whether modern governance would have made things even better or hampered his progress.

14 Charles Dunstone

Charles Dunstone was one of the earliest people who spotted the opportunity to build a retail chain around the mobile phone.

Carphone Warehouse cleverly made offering customer advice an integral part of its package. People of all generations, baffled by new technology, go to Carphone Warehouse for help and come out with a new phone.

Charles Dunstone has never been deterred by the risks associated with new technology. Others might worry about selling products that quickly go out of fashion, but he embraces each new product that comes to the market.

Charles Dunstone has been strategically astute with the development of Talk Talk and the merger with Dixons. In a fast-changing world he has shown a rare talent for predicting the future.

13 John Moores

John Moores was brilliant at spotting a market opportunity and showed a rare talent for turning good ideas into big businesses: Littlewoods football pools, stores and mail order.

To have developed three totally different businesses under the Littlewoods name was phenomenal. All three Littlewoods ventures appealed to the ordinary person in the street because John Moores had the ability to see things from the customer's perspective.

John Moore's achievement should encourage others to put their ideas into practice.

12 Charles Clore

Charles Clore was one of the first people to see the potential of undervalued property in other companies' balance sheets. Through a series of aggressive and contested takeovers Charles Clore built Sears Holdings into the UK's biggest retail conglomerate.

Charles Clore hired some exceptionally able retailers to deal with the detail, while he planned the next move and picked his next target.

Today, not nearly as many balance sheets contain undervalued freeholds but mergers and acquisitions will continue to be one of the main triggers that change the shape of shopping.

11 Simon Marks

Simon Marks took on a significant role at Marks & Spencer at the age of nineteen, immediately after his father's death. After a battle with his father's executors he became chairman at the age of 28.

Simon Marks introduced many of the ideas that became an integral part of M&S, including the St Michael brand and a sense of loyalty to both employees and the community.

Over the next 40 years, working closely with Israel Sieff, he turned M&S into a major force in British retailing with 7 million customers a week.

10 Ray Kroc

I have allowed an American retailer to invade my list because McDonald's have, since they opened their first restaurant in 1974, had a significant influence on how we shop.

Even if you don't like Big Macs (which I don't) or have never used a Drive-Thru, nearly 4 million other people call at a UK McDonald's every day and have got accustomed to the fast food way of shopping.

Forty years on McDonald's don't look or feel much different, but they are. Ray Kroc's successors have shown how to subtly keep a brand up to date.

9 Anita Roddick

With no retail experience or business training, Anita Roddick tried out a quirky idea and hit the jackpot.

The Body Shop has shown how a social conscience can put customers on your side and that having a fascinating person fronting a business gives the shops personality.

Everything about Anita Roddick's Body Shop fitted together. The shopfitting, promotion, product and sales staff all contributed to the image. The shops promoted the Green Agenda but they also took a lot of money. Like many husbands, I found The Body Shop a brilliant source of Christmas stocking-fillers and many experienced retailers learnt a lot from Anita Roddick.

Ian MacLaurin

It was Ian MacLaurin who changed Tesco from a cut-price food shop into a modern supermarket chain that regained its position as the UK market leader.

Ian MacLaurin listened to Tesco customers and through reducing checkout queues and encouraging branch staff to help customers navigate the store he persuaded customers to love the brand, because Tesco was on their side: 'Every little helps'.

Ian MacLaurin gained the initiative on price by scrapping Green Shield Stamps and built a land bank with the potential to beat other supermarkets in the rush to build out of town. He handed his successor Terry Leahy an excellent platform to develop a much bigger Tesco.

Ralph Halpern

Ralph Halpern performed a miracle when he transformed an ailing Burton business into the most vibrant chain in the UK.

He used the Burton property outlets to play a game of monopoly with Top Shop, Top Man, Dorothy Perkins, Evans and Burton itself, using shop design to give each fascia a strong image and individual personality.

For a decade Ralph Halpern dominated every shopping

centre and caused the rest of the retail sector to raise the standards of their shopkeeping.

6   Jesse Boot

From a single shop it took Jesse Boot only 35 years to build up a chain of over 550 chemists backed by major pharmaceutical manufacturing support.

His amazing vision and drive took advantage of changes in the law regarding the supply of medication and under the slogan 'health for a shilling' he developed a retail format that worked nationwide.

He recognised the importance of customer service and caring for colleagues, and most of all realised that his success depended on trust.

Jesse Boot created one of the most trusted names on the high street, which will probably prosper as long as his successors continue to comply with the caring culture he created.

5   Simon Wolfson

Simon Wolfson has quietly made Next a shining star of UK retailing and a trendsetter in the world of internet shopping.

He shows such sound judgement in forecasting the future and communicates the Next strategy so calmly it is difficult to believe that most of his trading is done in the volatile fashion sector.

Next made a dramatic debut in the days of George Davies, but Simon Wolfson has replaced the drama with standards of retailing that are the envy of the rest of us who have run a retail multiple.

4 Ken Morrison

Ken Morrison put his personal stamp all over his supermarkets and they worked, especially in his Yorkshire heartland. He knew his customers because he talked to them nearly every day and he knew how they wanted to shop for food.

Tesco, Sainsbury's and Asda have always been bigger than Morrisons but it was important for competitors to keep a close eye on Ken Morrison, whose individual style produced plenty of ideas worth copying.

Morrisons have struggled to take advantage of the Safeway acquisition or perhaps they have missed the magic touch of Ken Morrison. Whenever I visit a Morrisons store in Yorkshire I still feel the buzz that Ken Morrison brought to the business. His influence was that big.

3 John Davan Sainsbury

John Sainsbury had a remarkable record as the head of Sainsbury's. He floated the business in 1973 with a market value of £117m, and when he retired as chairman it was worth £8.1bn. During his stewardship Sainsbury's outperformed all his competitors.

John Sainsbury was at the helm when Sainsbury's were way ahead in the race to develop big out-of-town supermarkets. Bigger stores with much bigger turnover.

He had forward-thinking plans but still retained some old-fashioned principles. He was a regular shop visitor and a stickler for detail; everyone knew who was boss. John Sainsbury made Sainsbury's the market leader, but he was a difficult act to follow.

2 John Spedan Lewis

Many businesses have gone to enormous lengths to care for their colleagues, like Cadburys at Bournville and Lever Brothers at Port Sunlight, but none have made such a lasting impression as the Partnership scheme that John Spedan Lewis introduced to the Peter Jones and John Lewis department stores.

His success wasn't simply due to his enlightened employment practices. He followed a formula of good quality, low margins and great customer service which are still guiding principles for the 'Never Knowingly Undersold' John Lewis of today.

1 Marcus Sieff

Marcus Sieff ran Marks & Spencer from 1974 to 1984. It was the time when the rest of us regarded Marks as the gold standard of retail. We were envious of their culture with its reputation for value, quality, reliability and being a great place to work.

Marcus Sieff influenced most major retailers through his graduate training scheme which, as well as developing the next generation of Marks' managers, produced a lot of talent that won top jobs elsewhere. M&S training was the perfect passport to put on a CV.

Under Marcus Sieff's leadership Marks & Spencer became far and away the best retailer of the age. That's why he is at the top of my list.

INDEX